RETHINKING CELIBACY, RECLAIMING THE CHURCH

Michael H. Crosby

Wipf and Stock Publishers
Eugene, Oregon

Nihil Obstat:
Rev. Francis Dombrowski, OFMCap., STL
Provincial Censor of Books
June 17, 2003

Very Rev. Daniel Anholzer, OFMCap.
Provincial Minister
Province of St. Joseph of the Capuchin Order
June 19, 2003

Rethinking Celibacy, Reclaiming the Church
Copyright © 2003, Michael H. Crosby, OFMCap.

ISBN #: 1-59244-276-5

Wipf and Stock Publishers
199 West 8th Avenue, Suite 3
Eugene, Oregon 97401

Printed and bound in the United States of America.

In thanksgiving for communities of Capuchin Franciscan celibates who have nourished and sustained me in the Roman Catholic Church, especially those friars with whom I have lived at St. Benedict the Moor in Milwaukee: Kent Bauer, John Celichowski, David Schwab and Jerry Smith.

CONTENTS

INTRODUCTION

From the time I was born in 1940, I have always been a virgin, but I have not always been a celibate. Similarly, since the time I was ordained in 1966, I have always been a Roman Catholic cleric, but I have not always used power in a priestly way. The more I know about being celibate and being a priest, the more I believe both have value when freely chosen, but when they are connected by mandate, both can become destructive around the notion of power--especially when that power involves dynamics of control. Furthermore, when celibacy and priesthood are made inseparable by human fiat rather than divine decree (with its accompanying grace), even more serious problems will be found in the system that demands its priests to be celibate in a way that refuses any reasons to change it.

This realization has been compounded by the second wave of pedophilia scandals that have uncovered, not just abuse of power by some priests, but a deeper, systemic abuse of power by clerical leaders in the church at all levels. Given this background, while I will examine celibacy in our church and some of its problems (as well as its hopes) in this book, my probe also addresses this deeper problem related to the more systemic abuse of power used by the religious leaders who have mandated celibacy for its clergy.

First, as I examine celibacy in this book, I will show this gift involves much more than simply being a virgin. A virgin is one who has not had genital intercourse; it refers to a biological reality. Literally speaking, I am a virgin if being a virgin means not having "sexual intercourse with the opposite sex."[1] But celibacy represents something more profound. While including a biological dimension involving abstinence from genital intercourse, the "something more" about celibacy involves a stance that goes far beyond a dictionary definition as a "state of not being married," or "abstention from sexual intercourse," or even "abstention by vow from marriage."[2]

Interpreting celibacy as "abstention" or "non-marriage" reminds me of "John," a gay member of a religious order. He endorsed same sex intercourse among seminarians, priests and those in religious orders. He justified this position by saying: "I'm a virgin, because I've never had sex with a woman."

John's rationale for sex, even though he had vowed to be celibate, echoes stories heard later about priests in various African nations who were able to seduce nuns to have sex. Some more gullible sisters would submit to their advances after hearing them argue: "We are both consecrated celibates. That means that we have promised not to marry. However, we can have sex together without breaking our vows."[3]

With such confusion surrounding the meaning of celibacy and virginity, I am led to further nuance my opening remarks about celibacy and virginity: I am a virgin; I have never had genital sex with anyone, male or female. However, even with this nuance, it still does not mean I have always been celibate. In my experience of virginity and celibacy, the two remain very different. Thus part of the reason for this book.

I write this book not from any unhappiness as a celibate but from the deep conviction that the present dispensation of celibacy has resulted from historical factors that may have been necessary at one time. These historical factors contributed to the rise of patriarchal power in the Catholic Church. Both may have served their purpose; however now both are at counter-purposes vis-à-vis the good of the church itself.

The sources for my argument come from the way I have experienced celibacy in my own life, from listening to many others' experience as well as from conclusions reached from material gained from the internal forum (i.e., confession). It also has been influenced by the ways so many among the hierarchy seemed more intent on covering up the abuses that violated priests' and bishops' celibate commitment. But, above all, my thesis finds its main justification in a source much deeper than personal experiences, anecdotes and reports in the media. In the words of Jesus in Matthew's gospel, celibacy is a *gift,* not a mandate. Since Jesus' own words about celibacy ring truer and truer: "There will be few who can truly accept it," celibacy in the future must be freely made, not institutionally required.

I am convinced that when celibacy is no longer imposed, only a few, and especially only a few males, will accept it as their life-choice. When this occurs, Jesus' insight will be institutionally honored; it will be a rare exception when people "make themselves" eunuchs. When people freely choose celibacy their decision will have little or nothing to do with the tradition, law or practice of past centuries regarding a requirement for priesthood. It will not be connected to ministry or to orders. Rather it will result from a free choice arising from one's understanding of the force of God's reign in one's life and how that presence can be expressed wholeheartedly in the world. This will occur when celibacy becomes a "gift" rather than a "given." Then it will cease being used as an instrument of control to reinforce a patriarchal system that, in today's world, provides less and less meaning and even less justification.

This deeper system of control that demands celibacy has given rise to the second rationale that has led me to write this book. The current crisis around celibacy has made me conclude that this is the moment of grace given us by the Spirit to reclaim the Catholic Church for Jesus Christ and his gospel of liberation from all sinful forms of control. The time is at hand. The reign of God is near. Those who have promoted celibacy as a mean of control and exclusivity rather than a mandate of the heart dedicated to wholehearted service must repent.

Why I Decided to Write this Book

This book represents a thorough updating of a book I wrote in response to the first scandal of pedophilia that rocked the U.S. and Canadian churches in the late 1980s and early 1990s: *Celibacy: Means of Control or Mandate of the Heart?* My decision to re-examine the question in this book has led me to become of the need for a total reformation of the clerical structure of the Roman Church.

The first book began germinating during June 1993, notably at a triennial chapter of my province at St. Lawrence Seminary, Mount Calvary, Wisconsin. All perpetually professed members of the province were expected to be there. As we assembled, we were being barraged by allegations of pedophilia, sexual abuse and other sexual improprieties involving at least five Capuchin friars from our province, including some at the seminary. The day the chapter opened, *Time* ran an article in its "religion" section entitled: "The Secrets of St. Lawrence." Its subtitle brought the issue "out there" home to each one of us: "A Capuchin School Provides Catholicism's Latest Sex-Abuse Scandal." The article listed charges pertaining to two of our brothers who sat with us in that room. The provincial who had to respond to these allegations was pictured prominently.[4]

Outside the formal sessions I found myself in frequent discussions with other Capuchins. These conversations were evoked by the *Time* article, as well as from headlines in *The Milwaukee Journal* in late 1992 that gave detailed and quite lurid allegations of pedophilia and other forms of sexual abuse and impropriety done by our brothers at the seminary.

As we talked about these allegations and the way the papers reported them, I heard myself and other Capuchins say things that began to trouble me. Almost all of us, in very guarded ways, were alluding to our own past "non-celibate actions." These quasi-confessions were being expressed in comments that went something like: "Well, I've done many things that I don't want exposed in a headline in *The Milwaukee Journal*, but at least I've never fooled around with boys." The rationale seemed to be saying that, while our own actions might not have been able to be justified; they weren't as bad as what these brothers allegedly perpetrated.

The more I listened to what I and others were saying in our own defense, the more I began to hear louder than ever the first part of the sentence rather than the last: "I've done many things that I don't want exposed . . ." As I continued reflecting on this phrase, our approach to the problem increasingly seemed to suggest a kind of public way of cleansing ourselves of our own failures, even our own sins. It appeared to represent an admission on the part of all who said it, that we had failed as vowed religious to be the celibates we publicly had promised we would be. In these conversations, we all seemed to say we didn't want public exposure for our noncompliance with a vow we had publicly promised to observe.

Our guarded self-revelations led me to ask why none of us even feigned shock at what we were saying about ourselves. The general consensus seemed to be acknowledged that we all had failed in being celibate, at least sometime, in some way. This led me to wonder: If we Capuchin Franciscans—who supposedly have freely and publicly professed to be celibate men—were having such difficulties, what dilemmas must diocesan priests be facing, knowing that celibacy for them was not grounded in a supposed choice like ours but a law that Pope John XXIII said could be changed with the flick of a pen?[5]

Many people were hoping for a flick of the pen from one of Pope John's successors, especially when we experienced the first round in the "crisis of celibacy" which started in 1983 in the Diocese of Lafayette, Louisiana. Rev. Gilbert Gauthe was arrested and ultimately struck a plea bargain for sexually abusing dozens of children. It continued for a decade with a sweep that left few dioceses and large groups of male religious (like my own province) unscathed. This first round reached its most outrageous peak when James Porter was convicted. He admitted to molesting up to 100 children. It seemed to abate when wrongful allegations were made of Cardinal Joseph Bernardin in 1993 and recognized as such in 1994.

A seemingly isolated but very public glitch occurred when the Diocese of Dallas agreed in 1998 to pay $23.4 million to eight former altar boys and the family of a ninth who alleged they were sexually victimized by a priest, Rudolph Kos, in the 1980's and early 1990's.

All seemed relatively quiet for some years. Then, in 2001, reports long filed and unaddressed in Rome revealed more charges of pedophilia. In tandem, stories surfaced about clerical abuse of women, especially nuns in Africa. It had been recognized among church leaders that, in many parts of developing nations, especially in more rural areas, many priests had mistresses and children. Now even deeper abuses had to be acknowledged and addressed.

The stories that came to represent the second round of pedophilia narrations began in early 2002 with accusations that Rev. John Geoghan of the Boston Archdiocese had molested more than 130 children and that the Archdiocese had agreed to pay up to $45 million to scores of his alleged victims. When it became clear that he had been transferred by the diocese elsewhere with full knowledge of his past, a virtual tidal wave began of stories about priestly abuse, especially with pubescent boys. On July 23, 2003 the Massachusetts attorney general made public a 16 month investigation of the incidents. At least 789 children and probably more than 1,000 had been sexually abused by 250 priests and other church workers in the Archdiocese since 1940. Calling it "the greatest tragedy to children in the history of the commonwealth," the attorney general placed the blame directly on the leaders of the Boston Archdiocese.[6]

While this was shocking enough, what elicited the deepest outrage among people in the pews, as well as many outside the Roman Church, were story after story about institutional cover-ups by (arch)dioceses and religious orders of men. These covered situations across the United States from Boston to Los Angeles. Probably the most frightening expression came with the apology of Bishop Thomas J. O'Brien of Phoenix in June, 2003 for knowingly transferring priests accused of sexual abuse in exchange for being freed of being indicted by the local prosecutor, Richard M. Romley. The even more shocking thing about this incident was Romley's statement that: "We had been told that even if the bishop had wanted to resign, Rome would not allow it. That is, if he had been indicted, he would remain."[7] His resignation was accepted only after being arrested for a hit and run accident in which a man was killed.

The consequence of such exposés of priestly pedophiles in Europe and North America and abuse of women in some developing nation by clerics was inevitable: not only was there a call to end mandatory celibacy; what was not expected was the increasing and incessant demand to reform in the basic governance of the institutional church itself. However, even though by mid-2003, 21 bishops (all from Europe and North America except one from Argentina) had resigned since 1990 in the context of sex scandals, not one sign indicating the bishops recognized a need for change in those structures had come.

This seemingly incessant second wave of pedophilia charges (most dating to the first wave), with parallel revelations of ongoing episcopal mishandling, brings me to my second reason for writing this book: my deep disappointment in being part of a clerical system wherein power has been abused at the highest levels, even by well-meaning members of the hierarchy. This has led me to be convinced the whole system must change. Yet I fear these men have so insulated themselves ideologically and theologically, that they do not realize they have lost their moral authority; they still believe they are right in how they acted. This delusion keeps them from acknowledging any need for basic structural change. Given their isolated situation we can expect no change–in them. If change will come, it will be from a power source outside their clerical control and its culture.

Consequently, while this book aims to address the crisis related to celibacy in the Latin Rite of the Roman Church, it also seeks to challenge the system that refuses to address the issue. Setting up this lay-dominated commission or that professional review board to deal with allegations about clerical sexual abuse no longer will be enough, especially when the whole legal apparatus remains in the clerical control of those being challenged for their wrongdoing.

Given the limited (and disputed) data about the number of priests who are pedophiles, who are gay or who regularly violate their celibacy (which is limited, in good part, because of the bishops' refusal to initiate good studies about such), I will not be able to present my arguments from many "facts." However, this very paucity of data exposes the deeper issue that underlies this book: the resistance of church hierarchs in the United States and Canada, abroad and at the highest levels of the Vatican to truly investigate with good data the sexual orientation of its priests and its impact on celibacy as well as the number of priestly pedophiles and other sexual aberrations of its clergy. Why? For fear it will expose the need for radical change in the male, celibate, clerical model of the church.

With the second round of press stories about priests in the United States and other Anglo-Saxon countries committing sexual improprieties with children of the same sex and their confreres in less-developed countries impregnating nuns and taking them for abortions, it has become quite clear that huge concerns and contradictions related to the way celibacy is being lived exist in many parts of the Catholic Church today. Celibacy might once have been highly regarded, but, for many religious men and for many more diocesan priests, it simply isn't working. And, as long as it is imposed, it will be increasingly unworkable, unsustainable and unjustified. It is not needed for the church to function in a holy and healthy way.

A main reason the present dispensation about priests being male and celibate still obtains is not so much that it once might have been a necessary response to human aberrations but that, now, a few humans who are male clerics seem irrationally obsessed with maintaining what they call "the jewel of celibacy." In the process they seem ready to forego the traditional Eucharistic nature of the Catholic Church and, thus, undermine its core identity. In this obsession we have witnessed a form of abuse that is deeper and more systemic than the abuse of the priests who violated children here or nuns elsewhere. While not dismissing the individual stories of abuse by this or that priest here or abroad, it is this systemic abuse that needs to be addressed as well.

I don't believe you can say the 2% of priests (who most say represent the pedophiles in this country or elsewhere) constitutes any "pattern" of abuse. However a definite pattern of abuse has been revealed to be centered elsewhere. While, at the time of this writing, many of the nearly 200 (arch)dioceses had developed effective and transparent ways of dealing with pedophilia issue, hardly any were sufficiently open about past and potential problems about deception and abuse of power at the systemic level. There still is a resistance to admitting how aberrations of power reside in the patriarchal clerical structures which continually find intermingled the local parish, diocese, conferences of bishops, curial offices and the papacy itself. In none of these are there effective canonically-mandated checks and balances, openness and transparency, collaboration and consultation, much less open processes that demand responsiveness to efforts to change their dynamics "from below" or even "within." It is this "pattern" of abuse at the highest levels that has been exposed as the truly destructive reality that lies behind the second wave of allegations of clerical abuse of children (which, in the main, has been a rehash of allegations from the first round).

Individual priests who have been sexual perpetrators definitely violated the trust of their victims. However a deeper, systemic violation of trust by the leaders has elicited the current disgust on the part of so many in the church and outside the church. According to Peter Steinfels, author of the "Beliefs" column in *The New York Times*, the "current impatience, anger, and alienation" of so many has arisen, in good part,

> from the cumulative effect of years of irritations with what looks like the indifference, incompetence, or arrogance of church leaders. Embarrassing statements from on high, inept, ill-stated or ill-explained; embarrassed acquiescence at lower levels. Conservatives and liberals have different lists of complaints, to be sure. The center of gravity of the American Catholic populace is moderately liberal, which means believing that tolerance, pluralism, open discussion and inquiry, the equality of men and women, the ideal of intimacy in marriage, and many other typically "modern" values are authentic ways of living Christianity. For years these Catholics have felt, rightly or wrongly (and I believe, for the most part, rightly) that many high church leaders harbor an incomprehension bordering on contempt for this outlook. Other leaders, these Catholics sense, comprehend but comply, publicly endorsing positions that are privately questioned.

Steinfels concludes: "This underlying fissure between appearance and reality is why some scandals change history."[8]

My purpose in writing this book is to do what I can to help change the current history about mandatory celibacy and the abuse of power at the highest levels that sustains it. I want to show that, in too many cases, current laws about celibacy are often being violated, not so much because of selfishness or culture's decline, nor because of a breakdown of morality or the erosion of sacrifice, nor even because of society's promiscuity or consumerism. All too often, celibacy no longer obtains because of the law's own internal contradictions, its lack of grounding in solid scriptural reflection and spirituality, and the absence of a proper support system to support the truly celibate option. This is especially so for men.

The time for fear-imposed silence about mandatory celibacy and a male-only priesthood is over. The time for a system with leaders who demand that this silence be the norm must end. For the sake of those People of God who constitute the Roman Catholic Church and need the Eucharist, celibacy can no longer be imposed; it must be an option. Furthermore, the patriarchal clericalism that has demanded celibacy of its priests must be broken by the inclusion of women to full equality, including priesthood itself. Finally, in a reformed Catholicism which has reclaimed itself as the Church of Jesus Christ rather than one identified with the personalities (and clerical priorities) of this or that priest, bishop or pope (no matter how charismatic), the times demand the creation of new structures of authority and accountability, governance and guidance that honor the gifts of all the baptized in the fullest possible way. If in the early church there was a form of democracy that had bishops and pope accountable to the people, and if this gradually evolved to become a bishop-controlled aristocracy, the present institutional structure of the church has become a monarchy constellated around the papacy–the pope and the curia. We must now return to the best of what made us great–not in the eyes of the powerful of this world–but in fidelity to the message proclaimed by Christ and the early church.

We do ourselves a disservice by remaining in denial about the problems associated with celibacy that is imposed, to say nothing of the modus operandi of those leaders who do the imposing. Despite myriad data, as well as the deficits generated by financial payments to the victims of abusing priests and bishops, this institutional denial continues. It is sustained by a kind of delusion that arises when the leaders have found a way to believe the lies about clerical celibacy are "the truth." In response to this theoretical "truth," and because of the unfortunate paucity of hard data to reinforce my allegations, I have had to rely on a more anecdotal approach to discuss the issues addressed in this book. However limited, "facts" grounded in one's personal experience cannot be argued.

I have decided to take this approach hoping that this kind of honesty might help address what I believe is a problem that is much wider than celibacy that finds bishops afraid to raise the question, even as they close, merge or remove priests from more and more parishes. A saying goes: "We are as sick as our secrets." However, once a problem is admitted the secrecy is shattered and denial's control can no longer define the reality. Ecclesiastically speaking, this realization, hopefully, will help us work together for changes that may make us healthier individually as well as institutionally as Roman Catholics.

Outlining the Direction of the Book

With this background, this book's reflections are limited by my own social location as an able-bodied, white, male, straight, vowed, Roman Catholic priest who is part of an international congregation of brothers with a provincial setting in North America. Consequently, I will be the first to admit that my own privileged "social location" severely limits my viewpoint. Therefore, what I write may not reflect the horizon of people of color, women, gays, non-vowed or lay Catholics but it does arise from one who is "in the club."

The book begins by probing the traditional scriptural warrants for celibacy and the historical way celibacy has been used as a means of control in the church from the parish at the local level to the highest offices at the Vatican. I will argue that, while mandated celibacy may have arisen out of necessity and to address long-standing problems (i.e., to stop priestly offices from being passed on via familial benefices), it now is out of control and is undermining the possibility of truly being a church that is one, holy, catholic and apostolic. This will lead me to discuss current unhealthy ways priests have coped with celibacy. The result, for many, has been a crisis of meaning.

This personal crisis of meaning has now revealed a deeper, institutionalized crisis: a lack of faith in the patriarchal and autocratic system that demands it. I then will argue that the present way of institutional control vis-à-vis power, sex and religion in Roman Catholicism mirrors the kind of entrenched religious "system" that Jesus railed against. Given this biblical context, I will argue for the need to reclaim our church for Jesus Christ. Only in such a church honoring the charisms of all its members rather than the authority of its clericalized leaders will celibacy be able to be celebrated as the gift which Jesus said it would be. I will conclude the book by describing the kind of intimacy that will be necessary to sustain such celibacy.

I hope this book will not be considered another useless rant against celibacy or the hierarchy. I also hope that this will not be considered a diatribe against "the church" or disloyal to those religious leaders who have honestly tried to change what needs to be changed or those who, in their heart-of-hearts, believe the current dispensation is divinely-directed. Well-meaning as they may be (after all they only tried to preserve the system they inherited), their approach has created a crisis of meaning. A key to the problem is unmasking the way the Curia in Rome has come to control the whole institutional apparatus. If I contribute to help change the way governance is exercised in this church in a way that results in greater involvement, transparency and mutual accountability, I will be very happy.

Because the history of religious institutions shows that transformation rarely comes from within, I don't expect that my reflections will be met with much enthusiasm by those whose interests might be challenged by what I say. However, while I don't expect those in power will be open to my remarks, I will have the blessed assurance that I have done what I could.

This book is not my first attempt to offer a reappraisal of celibacy or pressure for a reform of my church. In 1991 I wrote *The Dysfunctional Church: Addiction and Co-Dependency in the Family of Catholicism.* In it I argued that a significant way of understanding some of the key institutional problems in Catholicism could be from the lens of viewing it as an addictive organization whose leaders were obsessed with preserving the male, celibate, clerical model of the church. This book moves beyond this analysis around addiction to a deeper grasp of the source of the problems in the institutional church as being grounded in dynamics related to abuse itself.

My next attempt to articulate the need for structural change came in 1996 when I wrote *Celibacy: Means of Control or Mandate of the Heart?* As the title itself explains, celibacy will be wholehearted only when it is embraced freely from within rather than being mandated from without. In this total revision of that book I also move beyond its analysis to show the deeper way power, sex and religion have all been united around mandated celibacy in the Latin Rite of the Catholic Church in a way that undermines its evangelical integrity.

The Inspiration of Francis and Clare for This Book: "Repair My House Falling Into Ruin"

I write this book as a priest of the Roman Church. I also write it as a member of a Province of Capuchin brothers and priests. In the latter vocation, I write inspired by the charism of Sts. Francis and Clare of Assisi. They felt called to live the Gospel at a period in the Roman Church when its leader was the most powerful pope in church history (Innocent III). Their way of responding now offers me an alternative vision of being church: a community of equals with acknowledged leaders who exist to serve the members in ways free of clerical control.

The Franciscan movement arose from words St. Francis heard as he prayed before the cross at San Damiano in Assisi: "Francis, go rebuild my house which you can see is falling into ruins." It was to this same incident and text that my Capuchin Franciscan confrere, Sean Patrick O'Malley, appealed when he "asked and pleaded" with the people of Boston after being named their Archbishop: "repair my church."[9]

Setting the context for this "falling into ruin" of the church, Francis' first biographer, Thomas of Celano, notes that, at this time, a deep sickness had invaded the church: "a deadly disease had grown up everywhere to such an extent and had so taken hold of all the limbs of many," including those who "take refuge under the mere name of Christianity" (i.e., the religion of the institutional church), that "were the physician to delay even a little, it would snatch away life, shutting off the life-giving spirit."[10]

While Francis envisioned a church reclaimed by the Gospel witness, his co-visionary, Clare of Assisi, was more constrained in the execution of her vision because she had to contend with the addictive disease at the highest levels of the church. It sexist vision of the Gospel poverty to which she felt called brought her to a life-long conflict with clerics at the highest levels. She was convinced that her call to live corporately in poverty just like the "brothers" was of divine inspiration. Consequently she resisted efforts of the Roman Curia to have her be defined in the traditional way of women religious of that day. Writing of her conflicts with Cardinal Hugolino, given as "Protector" of her Order (and who later became Pope Gregory IX), Sigismund Verheij writes:

> She was not going to be led off her course even by his supreme authority. When a papal decree made it practically impossible for the Friars Minor to preach the word of God to the sisters, she was so distraught that she dismissed the friars-almoners. She refused to accept food for the body [a protest known as holy anorexia] when the pope deprived her of the dispensers of spiritual food. Her sharp reaction led the pope to change his decree. Early on, she had 'fearlessly withstood him and refused to yield an inch' and accept his well-meant offer of material support. When he pressed further and offered to dispense her from her vow, her answer was clear and unequivocal: "Holy Father, in no way will I ever be freed from following Christ."[11]

As a follower of Francis and Clare and as a disciple of Jesus I believe the clerical abuse in more developed countries of "the North" (which has revolved around minors) and the clerical abuse of women, including nuns, in less developed places in "the South," both point to a more "deadly disease" that must be challenged. I don't think it will be found in any strong degree in those priests who have freely-chosen celibacy, be they gays or straights. Rather it will be manifested in the deeper pathology identified with the abuse of authority in the system that has used sex over the centuries in ways that have now been revealed to be unhealthy, unnecessary and, ultimately, unholy. The system must be changed if we are to become the church envisioned in the early writings which constitute the Christian Scriptures. This challenge to be the church of Jesus Christ rather than the church of the Curia, of this bishop or that local pastor who may try to say the church is "his," is necessitated because of the original challenge to convert that Jesus proclaimed to the threatened religious leaders of his day.

Today, possibly more than ever, Catholicism needs "the Messiah" to rebuild its institutional apparatus that has become too-overly identified with Peter and the Papal Curia to again become recognized as the church that the one Peter called "the Christ" heard was *his* church (Mt. 16:16, 18). In the process we need to ask Jesus to be faithful to his name and "save his people from their sins" (Mt. 1:21). Recognizing the sinfulness that has been revealed in the isolated but no-less-serious aberrations of a small percentage of the clergy but, at the same time, admitting the deeper sinfulness that has been revealed in a system of clericalized abuse that continues to violate women, demands admission of that sin, repentance of the sin and a firm commitment to amend or change the way of life heretofore canonized as divinely ordered. As we rethink what a healthy celibacy may be and, in the process, reclaim the Church for Jesus Christ, we hopefully will be witnessing individually and communally, congregationally and institutionally to his words: "Repent, for the kingdom of heaven has come near" (Mt. 4:17).

Chapter Notes

[1] "Virginity," Charles Earle Funk, ed., *Funk & Wagnalls New Practical Standard Dictionary of the English Language* (New York: Funk & Wagnalls Company, 1955), 1459.

[2] "Celibate," *Webster's Ninth New Collegiate Dictionary* (Springfield, MA: G. & C. Merriam Company, 1991), 219.

[3] Quoted in Marie McDonald, MSOLA, "The Problem of the Sexual Abuse of African Religious in Africa and in Rome," Paper for the Council of 16 in Rome, November 20, 1998. http://www.natcath.com/NCR_Online/documents/McDonald AFRICAreport.htm.

[4] Richard N. Ostling, "The Secrets of St. Lawrence," *Time*, June 7, 1993, 44.

[5] This statement of Pope John XXIII in a private talk with Etienne Gilson seems to have been printed first in *La France Catholique*, n. 862, 7-6, 1963). It is cited in Ruud J. Bunnik, "The Question of Married Priests," *Cross Currents* 15 (1965), 108-09. The exact statement has the Pope saying: "Ecclesiastical celibacy is not a dogma. Scripture does not impose it. It is even easy. . . I need only take a pen and sign an act, and tomorrow the priests who want to do so will be able to marry. But I cannot do it. Celibacy is a sacrifice which the church has taken upon itself freely, magnanimously, heroically. Recently I told the Cardinals, 'Can we allow it to pass that before long people will not be able to speak any more of the "one, holy, and chaste church?"' I cannot do it. No, I cannot do that."

[6] Thomas F. Reilly, quoted in Fox Butterfield, "789 Children Abused by Priests Since 1940, Massachusetts Says," *The New York Times*, July 24, 2003.

[7] Richard M. Romley, quoted in Charlie LeDuff, "Bishop of Phoenix Admits Transfers of Accused Priests," *The New York*

Times, June 3, 2003.

[8] Peter Steinfels, "The Church's Sex-Abuse Crisis: What's Old, What's New, What's Needed–and Why," *Commonweal*, April 19, 2002, 18.

[9] Sean Patrick O'Malley, quoted in Michael Paulson, "Bishop O'Malley Reflects Church's Changing Order," *The Boston Globe*, July 6, 2003.

[10] Thomas of Celano, "The First Life of St. Francis," 1, 9, in Marion A. Habig, ed., *St. Francis of Assisi: Writings and Early Biographies* (Chicago: Franciscan Herald Press, 1972), 230, 236.

[11] Sigismund Verheij, "Personal Awareness of Vocation and Ecclesiastical Authority as Exemplified in St. Clare of Assisi," trans. Ignatius McCormick, O.F.M.Cap., *Greyfriars Review* 3 (1989), 3.

CHAPTER ONE

The (Ab)use of Scriptures and Tradition in The Roman Catholic Church Regarding Celibacy

During the late 1980s, as part of my work toward a doctorate in theology at the Graduate School of Theology in Berkeley, I took a class on Paul's First Letter to the Corinthians. For one of the classes, I was reading chapters six and seven. Dealing with the end times, the text included Paul's reflections on virginity. At that period in my life I also was facing challenges--biologically, psychologically and spiritually. I was in my mid-years, the time when people reassess their lives and work, their sexually defined roles and commitments. Within this context I read the passage from Paul on celibacy:

> Now concerning virgins, I have no command of the Lord, but I give my opinion as one who by the Lord's mercy is trustworthy. I think that, in view of the impending crisis, it is well for you to remain as you are. Are you bound to a wife? Do not seek to be free. Are you free from a wife? Do not seek a wife. But if you marry, you do not sin, and if a virgin marries, she does not sin. Yet those who marry will experience distress in this life, and I would spare you that (1 Cor. 7:25-28).

Although my critical eye noted that Paul's letter was addressed to males (insofar as men are addressed in the second person "you," while women are referred to in the third person as "they"), the passage that struck me was Paul's opening words about virgins: "I have no command of the Lord, but I give my opinion."

1

"*Your* opinion," I found myself saying, as though I were challenging Paul. "I thought my being a celibate was God's will and now you say that you 'have no command of the Lord'!"

With that, deep rage arose within me. My anger got expressed in the words: "I've been duped." All along I thought I was "called" to be virginal, to be celibate, because this is what God wanted for me. And now I discover there has been no "command of the Lord" whether I remain a virgin or not--just that I be faithful to my baptism in whatever way would be best for me and God's people.

My anger at Paul then found me challenging the other rationale offered by Paul for being celibate: "Here you say it's only your opinion that people remain celibate, but that your opinion, 'by the Lord's mercy is trustworthy.' However, I don't place a great amount of trust in your opinion related to sex for various reasons. Primary among these is your own rationale in the text for why people should remain unmarried: namely, the nearness of 'the impending crisis.'"

To my surprise, almost as quickly as I felt such powerful rage, I found myself challenging myself with a surprising question: "Well, if you can't blame God or Paul, or anyone else, for being celibate, what are you going to do? You've got to find a reason within yourself rather than some external referent if you are going to stay. And if you can't find a healthy reason for your celibacy, you'd better deal with the consequences." This challenge led me to probe the various warrants around celibacy, including its treatment in the scriptures and development in the history of the Latin Rite of the Roman Catholic Church.

The Meaning of 1 Corinthians 7:25-28

Unlike the current crisis related to celibacy which has revealed a deeper predicament regarding the abuse of authority in the Roman Church, the "impending crisis" which influenced Paul's First Letter to the Corinthians arose from his conviction that the *parousia*, or the end of the world, was imminent. Since he believed Jesus was going to return very soon, it was better, Paul concluded, that people stay in their present situation of life. Although Paul accepted the fact that married couples would have sexual relations (1 Cor 7:2-6), he believed they should act as though they were not married (1 Cor 7:1, 7, 10). Thus his argument promoting celibacy had nothing to do with his commitment to celibacy as a value in itself. After all, he was a Jew and his background placed no inherent worth in a virginal life. In fact, it was considered a curse. On the contrary, his stance on celibacy arose from a worthy, but faulty belief the end of the world was nigh.

In the Hebrew Scriptures, celibacy receives little or no mention as a value. Although virginity is discussed, its value is viewed as a preparatory step to marriage (Gen 24:16; Jg 19:24). Indeed, when it is mentioned, virginity seems more identified with sterility than generativity. It reflects God's curse rather than God's blessing (Gen 30:23, 1 Sam 1:11, Jg 11:37). Its only positive meaning seems to have been connected with ritual purity (see Lev 21:7).

When celibacy was demanded as a religious stance, unlike now, it was required only for temporary periods, for instance when men would be in battle or priests would serve at the altar. The Jews' anthropology led them to believe there was something unclean connected to genital intercourse and women's menstruation; thus altar service necessitated abstinence (Ex 19:15; Lev 15:16ff.). The levitical codes demanded that, for cultic purity, priests refrain from genital relations with their wives prior to presiding at religious services (Lev 8:31-36; 22:1-4; 1 Sam 21:4). If they had such, they would become unclean; any resulting sacrifice thereby would be sullied.

According to rabbinic Judaism, every Jewish male was under the obligation to marry. Within the marriage the husband was obliged to have genital relations with his wife in order to propagate the race as well as to restrain from immorality. Men were encouraged to marry early, in their late teens or early twenties.[1]

Within these cultural codes, virginity and celibacy did find some adherents and advocates. Best known among these were some members of the Qumran community. However, again, the purpose of their celibacy revolved either around legally-ordered ritual purity or for great preparedness prior to battle. In either case, as the Rule of the

Community indicates, celibacy was not envisioned as a permanent way of life among any of Qumran's members.

This background helps us understand why Paul offers two different reasons for his pro-celibacy sentiment. The first reveals his preoccupation with the end-times. In light of the "impending distress" connected to the imminent *parousia*,[2] it was his opinion that "a person remain as he is" (1 Cor 7:26). Paul's second rationale flowed from assumptions related to the first, namely, that people should be totally oriented toward the last days. Therefore, he wrote, "I want you to be free from anxieties" (1 Cor 7:32).

While tradition has it that Paul seems to have been celibate (1 Cor 7:7-8), any "thorn in his side" notwithstanding,[3] his writings here as elsewhere indicate he lived under the conviction that a celibate's life was less troubled (1 Cor 7:28), less anxious (1 Cor 7:32), more ordered (1 Cor 7:35), and even happier (1 Cor 7:40).

Commenting on Paul's arguments (in a way that speaks to the issue of a celibacy that is imposed rather than suggested), Jerome Murphy-O'Connor has made clear that:

> Paul was convinced that his way of life was better than the married state. This made it inevitable that he should counsel others to do likewise (v 8), but he did not fall into the trap of imagining that what was best for him was best for everyone else. He was keenly aware of the danger of transferring a theoretical ideal to a concrete situation, and of the cruelty inherent in trying to create instant perfection by fiat.[4]

Given Paul's effort to find reasons why people should be celibate in light of the end of the world, one might wonder why he did not point to the value of modeling one's life upon that of Jesus, whom tradition has usually defined as a virgin and celibate. Despite the fact that, today, many members of the hierarchy try to make such a connection, Paul did not point to Jesus' celibacy nor did Jesus himself suggest his own assumed celibacy as a motive why others should embrace it. The only rationale, in their eyes, was for the sake of the kingdom which was about to come. It had to do something with God alone. This brings me to the second argument garnered from the New

Testament used as a rationale for priestly celibacy in the Latin Rite of the Roman Church.

The Meaning of Matthew 19:10-12

The context for the Matthean passage concerning Jesus' approach to what we call celibacy actually occurs as part of a deeper discussion on marriage and divorce: "Some Pharisees came to him, and to test him they asked, 'Is it lawful for a man to divorce his wife for any cause?'" (Mt 19:3). Their query precipitated Jesus' recollection of the traditional teaching on the divinely ordered indissolubility of marriage (Mt 19: 4-6). In retort they said, "Why then did Moses command us to give a certificate of dismissal and to divorce her?" (Mt 19:7). Jesus responded that it was because of the hardness of their hearts that "Moses allowed you to divorce your wives, but from the beginning it was not so. And I say to you, whoever divorces his wife, except for unchastity (*porneia*), and marries another commits adultery" (Mt 19:9). Hearing his reply, Jesus' disciples registered their consternation: "If such is the case of a man with his wife, it is better not to marry." To this Jesus answered, "Not everyone can accept *this teaching*, but only those to whom it is given"(Mt 19:10-11).

In his classic text on Matthew 19:10-12, Dom Jacques Dupont offers four interpretations regarding what Jesus may have meant by "this teaching." 1) The text refers to celibacy in itself, not as something for the aggrieved spouse in a marriage; 2) the text was meant for celibacy but was placed here by Matthew to serve as a contrast to marriage; 3) the "common" interpretation which sees celibacy as a particular gift from God; and 4) the teaching on celibacy must be seen in the context of 19:3-9 on marriage and divorce.[5] In my mind Dupont's fourth interpretation is the only way to understand the context of 19:3-9. Matthew's Jesus makes it clear in his teaching on the matter that divorce (except for *porneia*) and remarriage is never allowed.

Jesus' answer refers not so much to celibacy as we know it today as it has come to represent a demand for priests in the church, for religious and for gays, but to the status of the aggrieved party in a divorce situation. Indeed, this precise text is argued as why Canon Law demands that one must get an annulment from the first marriage that has ended in divorce in order to remarry. The context for this passage relates to how married people are asked to live when *porneia* is discovered in their partner and divorce results. As Jerome Murphy-O'Connor makes clear, "this passage has nothing to do with celibacy" in the sense that we now understand it.[6] Thus, to create legislation by appealing to a text that is unconnected to the rationale, calls into question any effective force of the legislation. Based on Murphy-O'Connor's insight that "Matthew 19:12 is not concerned with freely chosen celibacy,"[7] to make it the foundational imperative for compulsory celibacy is to abuse the sacred text for the sake of a tradition.

In applying the text to anyone who would be celibate, what is *given* ("the divine passive"),[8] first of all, has its origins in the divine donation, in God's gift; it has no source in any institutional mandate. Applied to today's situation that mandates celibacy for some, we can say that what is given, secondly, is not to all who would be priests nor to all those who were created homosexual; it will be for some of them but probably no more than for any other group of people. Just because a human institution has decreed it to be so does not mean God's donation will be so executed; this would place God's gifts under the control of human fiat. From the beginning of 19:11 and from 19:12 it is clear that Jesus envisioned celibacy as being totally voluntary; it cannot be compulsory or connected as a package with anything else. Celibacy has its own value and must be seen in that sense. As a value in itself it exists only for one reason: "for the sake of the kingdom of heaven" (Mt 19:12).

Matthew 19:12 also makes it clear that any celibacy faithful to the vision of Jesus must be freely chosen: "let anyone accept this" who so chooses. Celibacy can't be based on male superiority over women, on some kind of cultic purity connotation or to preserve an elite group to reinforce one's own interests. Neither can it be mandated for those whose God-given constitution orients them naturally to those of the same sex. Celibacy can only have scriptural validity when it represents a free response to the gift-experience of God's reign made present in the teaching and example of Jesus.[9]

Any God-given celibacy originates in a divine gift. Any divine donation can only come from God. It cannot be imposed by any institution. This is only natural since God, who naturally made people not to be celibate (Gen 2:18-25), would have to give a gift to those who would be celibate. The use of the theological passive ("to whom it is given") indicates that it is only because of a divine donation that one can be celibate in a permanent way of life. Consequently, previously accepted rationales raised to justify celibacy (such as "for the sake of being a priest," or "to minister in the church" or "for the reason that I made you homosexual") are inadequate and insufficient; celibacy can only exist for the sake of God's reign.

This insight helps us understand the next sentence of Jesus about "eunuchs." As he explains it in Matthew 19:12, there are three types of eunuchs. The first are those physically deformed "from birth." They cannot have genital intercourse. The second are those who have been castrated through the abuse of other men for the sake of their purposes of control, such as to serve as harem guards and courtiers (which is specifically rejected in Deuteronomy 23:1). Finally there are those who choose not to marry. They have made themselves so, not because they don't need intimacy, not because they have a repulsion toward sex or are genitally attracted only to people of their same sex, nor because they are repulsed by the idea of coupling. Their only reason for their celibacy can be that it is "for the sake of the reign of God" (see Mt 8:22; 1 Cor 7:17, 25-30).

Recent Papal Efforts to Find Alternative Scriptural Warrants for Celibacy

In 1993, despite the discrediting of the two main scriptural sources traditionally used to serve as warrants for celibacy in the Roman Church and despite the press barrage about clerical abuse, Pope John Paul II declared that "more than ever" the "church" was in favor of priestly celibacy. From his use of the word "church," it was clear the "church" he spoke about was not the peoples' church in the

United States, Canada or other developed nations where polls are taken: this "church" favored the idea of married priests by huge margins. With First Corinthians and Matthew no longer accepted as demanding celibacy as we know it, the sub-headline in *L'Osservatore Romano* commenting on the Pope's allocution intimated a new scripture text about to be promoted as a rationale for celibacy: "In the life of celibacy the Church sees a sign of the priest's special consecration to Christ as one who has left everything to follow him."[10]

Most exegetes have linked the "everything" that is abandoned with possessions, not including wives.[11] Although Luke places Jesus' visit to Peter's house (Lk 4:38-39) before Jesus' call to discipleship, both Matthew and Mark have this visit (Mt 8:14-15; Mk 1:29-31) after the call to discipleship. This indicates at least two things: Peter (at least in Mark and Matthew) did not leave everything, including his wife. Secondly, even after the call to discipleship, we find (again, at least in Matthew and Mark) Peter with a "house" big enough for his mother-in-law as well as his wife!

In his effort to find some Scriptural text to support his demand that priests be celibate and that there be no discussion against his position, the Pope seems unwilling to consider at least one other text indicating that the one our Tradition calls the "First Pope" and some of the other apostles appear to have had normal genital relationships with their wives *throughout their ministry*. In the same letter wherein Paul promotes celibacy as a way of preparing for the "impending crisis," he asks: "Do we not have the right to be accompanied by a believing wife as do the other apostles and the brothers of the Lord and Cephas?" (1 Cor 9:5).

When I first read about the Pope's statement regarding the "apostolic" basis for celibacy in 1993, I happened to be in Auburn, California. The news account appeared in *The Catholic Herald*, the Sacramento diocesan paper. Under the headline "Celibacy Rule is Reaffirmed by Pope," the CNS article stated:

> The Catholic Church has become more convinced throughout the centuries that celibacy is valuable for its priests and that

it follows Christ's design for the priesthood, Pope John Paul II said.

Priestly celibacy reflects Christ's call to his disciples to leave everything and follow him, the Pope said. "Jesus did not promulgate a law, but proposed an ideal of celibacy for the new priesthood he instituted." The ideal was affirmed with increasing insistence and consistency throughout the church's history, he said.[12]

Incredulous at the words and rationale for mandated celibacy I had just read, I called the diocesan paper and asked for a copy of the full text.

I had been taught that, on the one hand, Jesus never formally founded a "new priesthood" as such. Now our Pope was saying that Jesus not only founded a "new" priesthood, but a celibate priesthood at that! I could not believe the Pope was quoted correctly because his rationale seemed so far-removed from the scriptures and the early tradition of the Church. However, when the paper sent me the CNS text by fax, the statement was as quoted. Thus I found just one more example of a selective interpretation of the scriptures, misusing them to promote something far removed from their real meaning. Later we will see church teaching condemns such a practice.

Expanding the Passages on Celibacy to Their "Fuller Meaning"

Just because there are no formal scriptural warrants for celibacy as it has become mandated, especially for priests, one can't conclude that just because there is no clear exegetical support for celibacy as we now know it, there is no basis in the New Testament for celibates in the contemporary church. On the contrary, it is the task of each generation to find in the ever-creative word of God a message which speaks to its experience. In this sense, Sandra Schneiders writes:

> This implies that, when read from the vantage point of twentieth-century faith, standing within the tradition of the believing community, the gospel text will undoubtedly yield

more and richer meaning than the author was aware of expressing when he wrote it. This surplus meaning is not arbitrary, nor is every interpretation valid. But the process of validation consists in seeing the continuity of the interpretation with the direction of the author's intention and its coherence with the totality of the New Testament message as embodied in the lived faith of the community, rather than verifying that the interpretation coincides by identity with the explicit intention of the author.[13]

In all scriptural interpretive efforts, the key question is: What does it mean? Even though the meaning had one sense at one time, this does not mean a fuller, expanded meaning cannot be understood in later generations of people of faith. Therefore the question we must ask about the use of scripture texts such as 1 Corinthians 7:25-29 and Matthew 19:10-12 (especially the latter) is this: Even though the texts do not refer to celibacy as we know it today, can the rationales we know of today find reinforcement in the text?

Rewording the question in this way moves us from an untenable literal interpretation to a fuller understanding of a text that can nourish one's discipleship as a celibate. While I will expand on how this can be done in the last chapter, I believe we find a tentative answer when we consider the purpose that the two texts propose for celibacy. In Matthew it is "for the sake of the kingdom of heaven" (Mt 19:12); in 1 Corinthians it is to be "anxious about the affairs of the Lord, how to please the Lord" (1 Cor 7:32). In both cases one's life revolves around God. God's reign must ground all authentic celibacy if it is chosen as such in the church; it cannot be mandated. However, as the rest of this chapter shows, it has not been the case.

Celibacy's (Ab)Use in the Tradition of the Institutional Church

The two fonts constituting the Catholic Church are scriptures and tradition. We've already seen how the scriptures have been abused to reinforce mandated celibacy for priests. We now turn to the way the tradition has been abused to demand celibacy for priests as well.[14] In the process it will become clear that celibacy became institutionalized as part of an overall effort used and abused by clerical church leaders as a means of ensuring and maintaining their control.[15]

In his 1967 encyclical letter *On Priestly Celibacy*, Pope Paul VI declared: "Priestly celibacy has been guarded by the Church for centuries as a brilliant jewel, and retains its value undiminished even in our time when mentality and structures have undergone such profound change."[16] Despite the pope's words, celibacy's value as something mandated continually diminishes. Indeed, given the ongoing stories over priestly pedophilia in the developed world and revelation after revelation about clerical sexual domination of women in many developing nations, celibacy has not just been diminished; it has been seriously and permanently tarnished. Our current experience of this diminution and disintegration invites us to return to the sources to examine why the "brilliant jewel" of compulsory priestly celibacy has lost its luster despite the bluster.

While Pope Paul VI was right in saying that celibacy has been "guarded by the Church for centuries," in each of the four main periods of "the church" we find it promoted for basically the same reason: control. Celibacy was promoted during the fourth century when the papacy was beginning to exercise more control; during the period of the "Gregorian Reform" at the turn of the millennium when the papacy tried to break the back of lay investiture and concentrate power in clerical hands; around the time of Trent as an effort of the papacy to overcome clerical abuses and concubinage; and during the present post-Vatican II era when the papacy insists on preserving it even as more parishes go without the eucharist and more priests forced to accept celibacy are exposed, here and abroad, for violating it.

The result of this centuries-long effort has been the creation of a church characterized by a celibate culture. Its constitutive organization finds every significant element of church life under the control of the clerical group which is ensured through a hierarchical order. This has created two separate classes of cleric and lay with all power and authority, governance and guidance in the former. Philip Sheldrake notes:

> Those who belonged within the culture were empowered and those outside disempowered. As in all dominant power groups, the control of membership is crucial. Celibacy, in the limited sense of being unmarried, has long been a condition and proof of membership of a clerical class. It guaranteed, too, that the powers and possessions of clerical culture were not dissipated in a network of external relationships and in provision for heirs.[17]

1. *The First Period: The Rise of Celibacy as a Norm after Constantine*

From the time of the Apostles until the fourth century a balance of power existed in the way the church governed itself. A certain respect was evidenced in the power-sharing between the laity and the bishops. No celibacy-related restrictions were imposed on the clergy. Celibacy was a freely embraced option quite limited to groups known as "virgins" and "widows" (the assumption being, of course, that such were women). However, during this time, seeds of an anti-marriage, or at least an anti-sex attitude, were beginning to be sown.

Tertullian (ca. 150-230) declared celibacy was better than marriage and that sexual desires and delight, even in marriage, had no place if a marriage was to be considered Christian. Origen, his contemporary (ca. 185-255), believed that only a cessation of sexual activity would bring about life without death. Both Tertullian and Origen blamed women for luring men into sexual indulgence.

It was not too long before cultic sacralization harkened back to the very thing Jesus had rejected in his religion (see Mk 7:19): the appeal to the cultic purity of the Old Testament with its distinctions between what was considered unclean or clean. A champion of this thought, which demanded periodic continence for priestly service, was St. Cyprian (200-258). Paradoxically, while he promoted celibacy for liturgical service as early as the third century, and stressed the need for separation between clergy and laity, he also acknowledged the need for a certain balance of power between bishops and priests when he insisted in 254 that the people had the power to reject bishops they considered unworthy.[18]

Given this latter position, it should not surprise us that Cyprian clashed with Pope St. Stephen (254-257). It was Stephen who was the first to clearly appeal to the Matthew 16:18 text (the conferral of the keys upon Peter and the granting to him the power to bind and loose) to justify Rome's imposition on other dioceses.

Cyprian's "cultic purity" arguments based in Jewish Law began being raised in more earnest at the Council of Elvira in Spain, in the first quarter of the fourth century. The logic seemed to be: since Jewish priests in the Old Testament were required to abstain from genital intercourse at those times they performed altar service, Christian priests offering the perfect sacrifice at the altar should make the perfect sacrifice to achieve the perfection of purity. The effort to universalize this argument gained strength as daily mass began to come more in vogue by the end of the fourth century.

With the official recognition of the church in the Roman Empire, institutionalization and clericalization were not far behind–as well as a tendency to centralize power in an ever-decreasing number of hands. As the institutional church became "secular," the power of the clergy was extended in the effort to make priests "sacral." Paul Beaudette explains that:

> With the sacralization of the church, first of all, it was the clergy, rather than the martyrs and confessors, who became the bulwark against the *saeculum*, the "fighting line" against the world. Secondly, the church's establishment within the empire and the growth of asceticism meant that sexual continence, far from being one aspect of a "daily martyrdom," rose to prominence as its foremost expression.[19]

The nineteen bishops from the Iberian Peninsula at the Council of Elvira reportedly spent the majority of their time discussing whether celibacy was a more perfect state than marriage. A result of this was the first canon enacted in the early church which demanded celibacy of bishops, priests and all who serve at the altar: "It has seemed good absolutely to forbid the bishops, the priests, and the deacons, i.e., all the clerics in the service of the ministry, to abstain from conjugal relations and not to procreate children: whoever should do so, let him be excluded from the honor of the clergy"[20] The link of celibacy with "the honor of the clergy" also reveals a power/control dimension. A review of all eighty-one canons from Elvira makes it clear that this council recognized that clerical control over the laity was necessary and that celibacy would be the most effective way to establish this control. For priests already married, they were not to have intercourse.

Between this council and the first truly "ecumenical council," Nicaea, in 325, other local councils included various decrees related to the promotion of a celibate clergy (especially Arles and Ancyra, 314, and Neocaesarea, 314-325). The Nicene Council considered banning priests from marrying but, given strong opposition, decided against making such a universal decree. Indeed, fifteen years after Nicaea, the local council of Gangres declared anathema anyone who affirmed that people should not receive communion during a liturgy celebrated by a married priest.

In 385, Pope Siricius allegedly decreed bishops, priests and deacons should be celibate, including those who had wives. That his decree was not accepted, even by successive popes, is clear from the fact that other popes during this time themselves had children. Despite appealing to the notion of cultic purity to rationalize perpetual celibacy for priests ("All priests who want their daily sacrifices to be pleasing to our God must remain continually chaste"),[21] the deeper, but unstated, rational for this gradual imposition of celibacy upon the clergy became the main way of establishing papal control throughout the church.[22]

At the Council of Carthage (390), the bishops issued a decree which made the celibacy-cultic purity connection even more clear:

> The rule of continence and chastity had been discussed in a previous council. Let it [now] be taught with more emphasis what are the three ranks that, by virtue of their consecration, are under the same obligation of chastity, i.e., the bishop, the priest, and the deacon, and let them be instructed to keep their purity.... It pleases us all that bishop, priest, and deacon,

guardians of purity, abstain from [conjugal intercourse] with their wives, so that those who serve at the altar may keep a perfect chastity.[23]

Pope St. Leo the Great (440-461) extended the requirement of clerical continence to include subdeacons. Pope Gelasius (492-496), by claiming his right of dominance over all forms of civil power, developed a full theoretical justification for clerical dominance centered in the papacy. By the time of Pope Gelasius the notion of papal primacy as a dominant civil force had developed into a full theoretical justification for clerical domination. While distinguishing between religious power and civil power, he claimed supreme religious power for himself and his office. With him the term *pope* for the Bishop of Rome became normative.

Although Pope St. Gregory the Great (590-604) strongly affirmed celibacy, the succeeding centuries witnessed the discipline challenged, undermined, and generally disregarded. During this time the Latin Church allowed its priests to marry, but told them to practice celibacy within married life. Given the confusion which resulted, coupled with the impossibility of living with integrity in such a situation, the discipline fell into disarray and disrepute.

In response, many bishops and popes issued decrees trying to rectify the situation. Yet, as the bishop of Liege discovered, should he enforce the law of celibacy for his priests, he would have to dismiss his entire clergy.[24] Despite the efforts of various reform synods which insisted on celibacy, a practical kind of "don't ask, don't tell" rule took over. Lip service was given to the decrees, and discretion was asked lest there be public scandal.

In the sixth and seventh centuries, various councils tried to reform clerical corruption and the absolutizing tendencies of the papacy, but their efforts proved quite futile. Clerics continued creating new ways to maintain their positions at the local level while Roman popes played politics to ensure their own increasingly hegemonic power. An understandable result of this dynamic was the transfer of the locus of control from the laity to the clergy. In fact, as Peter Brown ably articulates, it represented the clergy as a group over and against the laity who supported it:

What made the history of the Christian Church notably different from that of other religious groups was the constant anxiety of its clergy to define their own position against the principal benefactors of the Christian community. Early Christians came to expect that their leaders should possess recognizable and perpetual tokens of superiority to the laity: they might be expected to give evidence of a charismatic calling; they were encouraged, if possible, to practice perpetual continence; even when both these criteria were lacking, only they had received due ordination through the "laying on of hands."[25]

2. *The Second Period: The Gregorian Reforms and Gradual Universalization*

Efforts to impose celibacy universally in the church increased with the election of Popes Leo IX (1049-54) and Gregory VII (1073-85). With the development of legislation directed by them and their successors in the late eleventh and early twelfth centuries, "the law of clerical continence was transformed into the law of clerical celibacy."[26]

Leo was imposed on the church as its leader by the German emperor Henry III. While he accepted the emperor's fiat, he also recognized the need to be faithful to the more democratic dynamic that characterized governance in the early church when he declared he would accept only if he would be approved by the clergy *and laity* of Rome. In an effort to address ongoing clerical abuses, he denounced simony (the buying and selling of spiritual offices and benefits) and, to stop it, insisted that subdeacons take a vow of chastity and that unchaste priests be excommunicated. Again, recognizing the power inherent in the laity, he also encouraged the laity to boycott any Mass offered by a married priest.

Leo surrounded himself with men dedicated to ensuring that celibacy would become the norm for all clergy. One of these was Peter Damian. For Peter incontinence was the chief clerical vice; the blame for such clerical deviations and lapses rested on women. In one of his oft-quoted sermons he declared of women:

> You vipers full of madness, parading the ardor of your ungovernable lust, through your lovers you mutilate Christ, who is the head of the clergy. . . You snatch away the unhappy men from their ministry of the sacred altar, in which they were engaged, that you may strangle them with the slimy glue of your passion. . . The ancient foe pants to invade the summit of the church's chastity through you. . . You suck the blood of miserable, unwary men, so that you might inflate into their innermost parts a lethal poison. They should kill you. . . for is there any hand with sacred chrism that you shake with fear not to touch, or oil that you do not defile, or even pages of the gospels and epistles that you do not use familiarly [in an obscene way]?[27]

Leo was succeeded by a series of short-reigning pontiffs. Although many of these continued to be influenced by Peter Damian, they did not achieve any great reforms of the clergy or changes in the celibacy rules. On the contrary, their pontificates are notable for the presence of a countervailing force to the increasing effort to make the clergy celibate. A representation of this is found in the person of an Italian bishop, Ulric of Imola, who lived in the middle of the eleventh century. The main thrust of a "rescript" he allegedly wrote was to condemn the decrees of Nicholas II regarding clerical continence as unjust and impious, non-canonical and indiscreet. He argued that one of the main effects of compulsory celibacy would be to drive the clergy into homosexual relationships. He concluded that the imposition of celibacy violated nature: "Since therefore the good of continence, indeed every good, is the gift of divine grace alone, capable of being embraced neither through mandate, nor through one's own free will, they not only err but indeed they labour in vain, who attempt to force chastity on these men."[28] Ulric also scored those who distorted the scriptures seeking to justify the rule of celibacy as "straining the breast of scripture until it yielded blood instead of milk." Not surprisingly such deviations from what was becoming the norm were enough to merit his solemn condemnation at a council in 1079.

One of Pope Leo's chief councilors was Hildebrand. When he succeeded him as Pope Gregory VII, the reputation of the priesthood seemed to have reached, until then, rock bottom. The clergy had become effectively secularized and feudalized; priestly candidates were often chosen more for their loyalty to a human lord than any divine authority. Those in the married clergy considered their offices to be hereditary; church endowments enriched priestly families. Such dynamics now had created entire priestly dynasties of clerical bureaucrats. Married priests and bishops often treated their ecclesiastical offices as family property. They converted any sacred dignity they had into family heirlooms.[29] Increasingly, the people demanded to be freed from the evils of such clerical aberrations.

In a heroic effort to control this increasing clerical corruption, Gregory decreed that no one could become a cleric without having made a vow of celibacy. Furthermore he forbade all the laity to participate in any religious service celebrated by any married clergyman be it subdeacon, deacon, priest or bishop. Revealing Peter Damian's misogynous influence on his thinking, Gregory wrote that "one cannot touch both the body of Christ and the body of a whore."

Gregory tried to build on Leo's effort to bring about a serious church-wide effort to reform clerical abuses connected to being married. Particularly, these abuses revolved around lay investiture and simony. Their effort to impose celibacy as a way to redress the wrong had a powerful side-effect: an ever-increasing centralization of clerical and papal control in the church. By addressing clergy abuse with the celibacy command, the papacy could concentrate its own power. As in any control-defined situation, fear and intimidation were the rules regarding dissent: Gregory demanded that all in major orders live in clerical households, support each other in "moral purity" and report on any deviant behavior among fellow clergymen. The result, Bernard Cooke has written, was that:

> At every step of the way, the extension of clerical celibacy and its establishment finally as universal discipline was a matter of legislation and enforcement by means of threat and

coercion, rather than by way of convincing through intrinsic argumentation or inspiration. . . [T]he institutionalization of clerical celibacy came through law and sanction, and was effectively imposed only when church authority became absolutely monarchic (and effectively so) under Gregory VII and a succession of powerful medieval popes.[30]

Despite the efforts of Leo and Gregory, their decrees were not universally embraced. Thus, in 1119, at the Council of Rheims, Pope Callixtus II oversaw a decree that married clergy would be expelled from office and excommunicated if they continued to live with their wives. The argument for the discipline of practical celibacy was grounded in a link with the priest's cultic role. Again, not far below that rationale was the deeper issue of control itself, be it the pope's control over priests or priests' control over the people at the local level. As Barstow writes:

> Gradually the clergy were being more closely controlled by their bishops who were, in turn, more tightly supervised by Rome. The priesthood was being set further apart from the laity, who had begun to insist on a celibate ministry. And, as this happened, the priesthood's power through the sacraments, especially of confession and penance, began to increase.[31]

The First Lateran Council (1123) forbade the clergy to marry. Those in marriages were ordered to dissolve them. Although some debate whether the First Lateran Council actually made marriage for priests invalid, in 1135 the Synod of Pisa for the first time declared that marriage was impossible for a cleric in major orders. Pisa's decree was appropriated into the decrees of the Second Lateran Council in 1139. Succeeding councils, as well as collections of decrees (gradually becoming what is known as "canon law"), increased the demand for clerical celibacy. The apogee of the effort of the decretalists came in 1140 with the publication of "Gratian's Decrees," the forerunner to modern canon law. Canonists succeeding Gratian justified clerical celibacy on the grounds that the vow of celibacy was inherent in the sacrament of orders itself.

Despite such decrees buttressed by statements of councils and popes, one need only examine the practices of some of the popes to see the opposite. Parish priests could feel justified in pursuing women insofar as they were emulating popes like Alexander VI who fathered many children. Not surprisingly, in fifteenth-century Burgundy, half of the children born out of wedlock for whom legitimation was asked, were children of priests. In the words of church historian Daniel-Rops: "Rome had set the example of a scandal whose repercussions were felt in the most distant corners of the church."[32] Such aberrations begged for reform.

3. *The Third Period: Trent and Succeeding Centuries*

The Reformation represented a reaction against the cultic priesthood and the imposition of celibacy as a manifestation of clerical control; at the same time, however, it also represented an effort to return to the Jesus Christ of the Scriptures as a way to challenge the abuse of power that had been consolidated in the Roman papacy and hierarchy over the centuries. Rather than emulate this "Protestant" effort by its own conversion, the counter reform led by the clerical forces who gathered at the Council of Trent (1535-1563) reinforced dynamics related to celibacy for priests and disciplines related to institutional control. The counter-reformers reiterated the ban on marriage for priests and the superiority of virginity to marriage, arguing for the latter on grounds of cultic purity. Marriage and priesthood were mutually exclusive. The former represented the profane; the other the sacred. In 1563 two canons (9 and 10) were approved that represented this thinking:

> If anyone says that clerics in sacred orders or regular clergy who have made solemn profession of chastity can contract marriage and that the contract is valid, despite the law of the church and their vow notwithstanding, and that the opposite opinion is nothing but a condemnation of marriage, or if anyone says that all those who feel that they do not have the gift of chastity (even if they have vowed it) can contract marriage: let him be anathema. For God does not deny the gift to those who petition for it in a correct manner, nor does he permit us to be tempted beyond our strength.

> If anyone says that the marriage state is to be preferred
> to the state of virginity or of celibacy, and that it is not better
> and holier to remain in virginity and in celibacy than to be
> joined in marriage (see Mt 19:11f; 1 Cor 7:25, 38, 40); let him
> be anathema.[33]

While Trent attempted to ground its rationale for clerical celibacy in the traditional scriptural passages, it did acknowledge that its requirement for it arose not from doctrinal beliefs but from discipline. This gave rise to one of the unique wordings emanating from the ninth canon of Trent: the notion of "gift" in connection to celibacy. The council also marked one of the first times official teaching indicated that God would grant the grace of perseverance in celibacy to those who asked. It declared anathema any who said that clerics who felt they did not have the gift of chastity could marry. This teaching prevailed for centuries. It was codified in the 1918 Code of Canon Law.

Another result of such decrees can be found in the ever-increasing concentration of power and control over the people by the local clergy, over the parish priest by the hierarchy, and over the bishops by the pope and those surrounding him. J. D. Crichton notes that, by centralizing authority among the clerical caste: "the juridical emphasis became ever greater and the growth of the pyramid church ever more irresistible."[34] With Trent, the clergy effectively became identified more with power and control than preaching and proclaiming God's reign. They would be the front lines in ensuring clerical control would characterize the entire institutional apparatus.

From the seventeenth century on, inspired by the "French School" of leaders like Pierre de Berulle, a gradual shift began taking place from identifying a priest around his cultic role to his mystical representation of Christ himself. Berulle's influence was great in redefining the priest as someone set apart from the laity. The Enlightenment, another French-inspired movement, reached its peak in the French Revolution. The post revolutionary era represents the last time a general dispensation from clerical celibacy was authorized. Beaudette notes:

When the Constitution of 1791 provided that no profession could debar a person from marriage and that no public official or notary could refuse to ratify a marriage on such a ground, the French clergy was split in two, with marriage being considered a pledge of loyalty to, and continued celibacy a silent protest against, the new regime. After the Reign of Terror, one of the first efforts at reorganizing the church was directed at the restoration of celibacy. Following the signing of the Concordat with Napoleon, which left the internal discipline of the church to itself, 3224 priests and religious petitioned either for reinstatement or for the regularization of their marriages. Of these over 2000 chose the latter. The arrangement . . . reducing clerics to the lay state and validating their marriages marked the. . last time in modern history that the church has authorized a general dispensation from the discipline.[35]

Striking parallels exist between the post-revolutionary period and post-Vatican II. In both cases one must ask: Was it for power and prestige due to being part of a clerical caste that influenced men to become priests? Did they take on celibacy to be part of a clerical caste? It would seem that these possible rationales helped people forego marriage until marriage came to be valued as a good in itself (as with the Revolution) or in better theology and phenomenology (as with Vatican II) and the rise of pluralism and secularism. In both cases, the result was the same: a mass exodus from the clerical to the married state.

The final stage in centralizing church power around the papacy came with the First Vatican Council. On July 18, 1870, the *Constitution on the Papacy,* with its section *Concerning the Infallible Magisterium of the Roman Pontiff* was approved by an overwhelming majority of the assembled bishops. Most bishops disagreeing had already left Rome for fear of public disagreement. From now on, anyone questioning the almost absolute authority of the Pope to demand assent on almost anything he said, would be held suspect.

With this action, a church that once governed itself around quite democratic principles, now had moved from being aristocratic in its governance. Gradually, and for the future, what had become an episcopal aristocracy evolved into an almost absolute monarchy.

4. *The Fourth Period: Post-Vatican II Priestly Celibacy and Institutional Control*

At Vatican II Pope Paul VI insisted that any public discussion of celibacy at the Council was "absolutely inopportune." While this idea was not challenged seriously by the conciliar fathers, a notion that did get dismissed was the justification for clerical celibacy that appealed to cultic purity. By that time, enough good scholarship had penetrated the ideology of those writing the documents and proffering rationales for priestly celibacy, and the argument lost its former credibility. Despite this fact, the Decree on the Training of Priests still urged candidates for the priesthood to "recognize the greater excellence of virginity consecrated to Christ."[36] However it did not clearly state that this "greater excellence" established virginity above marriage.

But patterns do not die easily, especially when cultic purity appeals promoting clerical celibacy get exposed as a way of proving sacral support for patriarchy. Overtones of cultic purity for priests demanding celibacy began getting resuscitated as a main rationale for the discipline of celibacy in a statement of Pope Paul VI February 2, 1975. In it the pope referred to the fact that priests and members of the consecrated life were celibate to maintain a "purity of the body."[37] More recent attempts being made to justify celibacy have made similar appeals to cultic purity as well.

Despite such efforts, the ultimate rejection of the cultic purity reason for priestly chastity has produced an unforeseen consequence. If the main reason used to justify a practice is discounted, what will the rationale be to continue that practice? Hanz-Jurgen Vogels has argued that the illogic of the rationale--which was used for centuries to justify the discipline--now calls into question the disciplinary laws that were made based on this justification.[38] Vogels asks, "Can the celibacy law then bind the conscience when its original basis and moral aim, the 'purity of priests,' has been recognized as mistaken and has seemingly not been replaced by any new basis on which to justify so far-reaching an obligation?" Arguing from the dictum that states, *cessante causa cessat lex*, Vogels concludes: "If the objective of keeping priests from 'impure' activity within marriage has disappeared--and in fact nobody dares to repeat the original motivation of the law--then we have to ask whether the law has any compelling force at present."[39] If the core reason for a law no longer holds, that law seems to lack juridical foundation.

With the discrediting of the "cultic purity" arguments and the Second Vatican Council abrogating the "virginity is better than marriage" argument with its universal call to holiness, a new rationale to justify priestly celibacy was needed. This was found in Trent's notion of God giving the gift or charism of celibacy. Now Matthew 19:11-12--with Jesus' words about it being "given"--would make their way into a conciliar decree. Without noting that this passage was written before anything such as priests as we know them existed, priests now were told to ask God for the grace of the gift to fulfill their promise to live a celibate life. This argument underlies the rationale proffered by the Second Vatican Council.

The council admitted that celibacy is not "demanded by the very nature of the priesthood, as is evident from the practice of the Eastern Churches." Furthermore, it said the council "in no way intends to change that different discipline which lawfully prevails in the Eastern Church." However, with another appeal to the Matthean and Pauline texts, the Decree on the Ministry and Life of Priests concluded of mandated celibacy for the clergy in the Latin Church: "It trusts in the Spirit that the gift of celibacy, which so befits the priesthood of the New Testament, will be generously bestowed by the Father, as long as those who share in Christ's priesthood through the sacrament of orders, and indeed the whole Church, humbly and earnestly pray for it."[40]

Like previous efforts to provide scripturally grounding, the rationale considering celibacy to be a "gift" appears to be fraught with internal contradictions. The first contradiction deals with the difference between something imposed and something offered freely, between something institutionally mandated and something chosen from a sense of being called. The second contradiction can be termed a *deus ex machina* or a *post hoc, ergo propter hoc* argument which, in effect, states that someone asking for the grace will get it. It's as if we can control God to give a grace because we ask for it, even when it may not be God's chosen grace for us!

In asking the priest to pray for the gift of celibacy, the council seems to accept the fact such a "gift" cannot come through the law but through prayer. But if a priest does not pray for the gift, one might ask: from where will the "gift" of celibacy come? From the law? The contradictions in this rationale seem clear. This "ask and you will receive" celibacy rationale that seeks to address the law-gift dichotomy has led Vogels to conclude:

> But the Spirit has already shown us, in scripture and tradition, where we have to look for a solution to the crucial problem of gift and law. According to the New Testament, the charisma cannot be obtained by prayer, and this was confirmed indirectly by the Council of Trent when it did not expressly include the ability to obtain it by prayer in its definition.[41]

In 1983, the Revised Code of Canon Law, stated clearly the real reasons for priestly celibacy: "Clerics are obliged to observe perfect and perpetual continence for the sake of the kingdom of heaven and therefore are obliged to observe celibacy, which is a special gift from God."[42] A breakdown of this sentence reveals two threads: an ecclesiastical demand and a scriptural warrant. Clerics are bound to observe perfect and perpetual continence and are obliged to live in celibacy. This continence is for the "sake of the kingdom;" this celibacy is "a special gift from God."

In June, 2003, the Vatican reaffirmed celibacy for priests, rejecting any arguments that part of the crisis in the priesthood could be reversed by opening the priesthood to married men. Instead, it argued, current priests should better explain the priesthood to others. This fiat came despite the fact that, according to Vatican statistics, in 1978 there were 1,797 Catholics for every priest; in 2001 there were 2,619. With this reiteration of the demand for celibacy for diocesan priests, it became clear the Eucharist could be sacrificed on the altar of clerical celibacy.

The Historical Result: Mandated Celibacy as
More Important than the Eucharist

With the core arguments which historically have been used to justify clerical celibacy de-legitimated, we face a crisis in the theology used to justify clerical celibacy as well as a crisis arising from its aberrations in the form of clergy abuse. In an effort to change the focus of the debate, the papacy now says the crisis regarding the priesthood does not derive from clerical celibacy but in the decadent culture wherein it must be lived. That our culture, embedded as it is in capitalist forms of control, is decadent will get no argument from me. But the real cultural culprit that is decaying can be found in the clerical culture itself, the patriarchal system demanding it and the curial forces that insist on its continuance. Unacknowledged, the result to be anticipated can only be more clergy abuse whether it be Internet sex or same sex abuse of minors in the United States or abuse of women, including nuns, in places like Africa as well as the system that sustains it. There also will be a declining numbers of truly healthy candidates and an ever-shrinking pool of priests to celebrate the Eucharist. It has become evidently clear from the fiats of Rome regarding its insistence that priests at Eucharist be celibate in the Latin Rite that what they say must be done is more important than Jesus' command that the Eucharist be celebrated.

As long as celibacy is used in the Roman church as a means of control, it also will be abundantly clear that the hierarchy's underlying preoccupation is not about feeding the flock the eucharistic bread. It will become more evident that, whether out of poor theology, history or fear, it will be willing to deny people the eucharist to preserve the celibate priesthood. This will be done in face of the evidence that a change in the celibacy laws would bring in more candidates for the priesthood, including a return of those who left the active priesthood because of the legislation.

Without even addressing the issue of women priests, the ordination of married men would solve the clergy-shortage problem. According to Dean Hoge writing as far back as 1987:

the celibacy requirement is the single most important deterrent to new vocations to the priesthood, and if it were removed, the flow of men into seminaries would increase greatly, maybe fourfold. Therefore this option provides a solution to the shortage of priests. As we said earlier, if celibacy were optional, probably the number of Catholic priests would increase over a period of years until it hit a financial limit, that is, until as many priests were in service as the Catholic community could financially support.[43]

The obligation to provide the eucharist is more critical to the life of the church than to protect the interests of those who insist only celibates be the celebrants of that eucharist. In this sense, the words of Karl Rahner ring true: "If the church everywhere or in certain areas is unable to find enough clergy unless she abandons celibacy, then she must abandon it; for the obligation to provide enough pastors for the Christian people takes precedence over the ideal, legitimate in itself, of having a celibate clergy"[44]

Rahner's conclusion arises from the conviction that the sacraments exist for the people rather than the preservation of a celibate clergy. Despite polls showing the people's openness to married priests and women priests, the papacy has closed its eyes to the data and closed its ears to those who cry for more regular access to the eucharist; it has hardened its heart. Why? Cardinal Jan Schotte, a Curia member, summarized it well. The issue is not issues around sexuality as much as it is around power: if the Pope and the bishops would be accountable to the people it would "threaten one of the Pope's most precious prerogatives, his sovereignty."[45] Whereas once the reign of the Bishop of Rome was grounded in the peoples' ratification, now accountability to the people has become a threat to his "sovereignty." Given its refusal to reflect the give-and-take that characterized governance in the early church, we also can ask: Why does the papacy insist on a male-only clerical celibacy when there are no scriptural warrants demanding it? And, having examined tradition, why is it that a key reason for its institutionalization–namely the need to control transfer of estates–no longer exists? In fact, today it just may be that the singular control of the monies in many dioceses incorporated with the bishop as corporate soul has brought many of them near to bankruptcy to pay for abuse cases.

It has become increasingly clear to me that the current crisis in our Church cannot be attributed to the clergy, the abuse of their promises related to celibacy or anything else, as much as to the leaders who refuse to confront the lack of scriptural warrants for celibacy, the tradition has been used to effectuate control by clerics at every level of the church and the consequent inability of the wider church to faithfully celebrate in ritual Christ's command to achieve its identity as his living body in the eucharist. I have come to believe, in a paraphrase of Paul to the Corinthians, that if the leaders continue to keep God's people from coming together to celebrate the eucharist by insisting that only male celibates can preside, they will be bringing judgment on themselves (see 1 Cor. 11:29). To maintain the tradition of clerical celibacy when there are not enough priests to be with the people that they might fulfill the words of Jesus "Do this in remembrance of me" (1 Cor. 11:24) is also to incur the condemnation of Jesus addressed to earlier religious leaders who would not change their ways: "So, for the sake of your tradition, you make void the word of God. You hypocrites! Isaiah prophesied rightly about you when he said: 'This people honors me with their lips but their hearts are far from me; in vain do they worship me, teaching human precepts as doctrines'" (Mt. 15:7-9).

On the Non-Ordination of Women

Monday, May 30, 1994 was Memorial Day in the United States and a memorable day in the church. This was the day that Pope John Paul II issued a letter to the bishops declaring "that the church has no authority whatsoever to confer priestly ordination on women and that this judgment is to be definitively held by all the church's faithful."[46]

The wording of the statement revealed a new dimension of Roman decrees related to women's (non)ordination: anyone dissenting invited dismissal from the church itself.[47] Cardinal Joseph Ratzinger said that anyone who did not give obedient assent to the

statement "obviously separates himself from the faith of the church."
Further discussion was ruled out; there would be no more debate on
the subject. The case was closed. This led *The Tablet* of England to
editorialize:

> The cardinal has a duty, of course, to make clear the status of
> the Pope's letter without ambiguity, but it sometimes seems
> that the Catholic authorities do not understand how this
> language of centralizing control and imposed authority, which
> has become characteristic of the present Roman tone, is heard
> inside and outside the church, and what sort of impression it
> gives. The present emphasis is on a comprehensive and
> complete system of doctrines enshrining the faith and a
> complete system of prohibitive laws which oblige under all
> conditions.[48]

In his apostolic letter Pope John Paul II also referred to
previous statements issued by Pope Paul VI. The latter argued for
male-only priests from the fact that Christ chose only men as apostles,
the constant practice of the church which imitated Christ in choosing
only men, and the church's "living authority which has consistently
held that the exclusion of women from the priesthood is in
accordance with God's plan for his church."[49]

Pope John Paul II's reference to God's plan for *his* church
reflects a current cultural conditioning that still has not been
recognized as historically determined. Unwittingly, such wording of
the apostolic letter shows how deeply patriarchal cultural
conditioning has penetrated the minds and language of the hierarchy.
The depth of their resulting inability to see also becomes quite clear
when Pope John Paul II insists, with Pope Paul VI, that "Christ's way
of acting did not proceed from sociological or cultural motives
peculiar to his time."[50] Given the depth of the power of language to
influence stereotypes, these popes were not able to recognize how--in
referring to God as *he*--their own words reflect sociological and
cultural conditioning. Consequently their own interpretation of the
Jesus of history seems bound to be conditioned by that very limited
perspective as well.

With such "non-culturally-conditioned" reasoning given as a rationale demanding the people's unconditional assent and the decree about the non-debate on the issue of women as priests, a Vatican overview of the apostolic letter concluded:

> Therefore, since it does not belong to matters freely open to dispute, it always requires the full and unconditional assent of the faithful, and to teach the contrary is equivalent to leading consciences into error. This declaration of the supreme pontiff is an act of listening to the word of God and of obedience to the Lord on the path of truth.[51]

Linking the Pope's statement with the "path of truth" strongly intimates some kind of infallible truth. But, given the patriarchal foundation of this "truth," its limitations seem increasingly clear: in the Pope's own words, it represents the "truth of man." Unfortunately this "truth of man" seems limited precisely to the truth of "man" rather than the fullness of truth which comes from the truth of man *and* the truth of woman, much less the truth that is God.

Eight years later, when Pope John Paul II convened a meeting in Rome with the U.S. Cardinals, Cardinal J. Francis Stafford, said that the meeting would include the beginnings of an important discussion about the roots and the role of priestly celibacy: "If it's something that developed simply in the 12th century for unworthy motives like inheritance," he said, "then it's difficult for me to see it being sustained," he said. "But if celibacy is of apostolic origins and has important connections with church tradition," he concluded, "then this experience in the U.S. is not going to undermine that."[52]

As the U.S. Cardinals and others prepared to go to Rome to discuss the second wave of reports about clerical pedophilia at least one indicated that the issue of priests being allowed to marry would be discussed. A few days after that, at a meeting with some bishops from Nigeria (which itself has a high percentage of its priests who, as clergy have produced children), Pope John Paul II insisted that the issue would not be allowed to be discussed. Not one bishop seems to have dissented. Instead any dissent noted would be that coming from the curial forces that insisted in the final document that a tougher line should be taken against "individuals who spread dissent and groups which advance ambiguous approaches to pastoral care," all code words and phrases for those who disagree with curial decrees.[53]

The power of the Curial forces to silence even cardinals brings me to the next chapter. It will address the fearsome power its member have accumulated to the point that they now possess a kind of monarchical power accountable to none but the Pope himself.

Chapter Notes

[1] Harvey McArthur, "Celibacy in Judaism at the Time of Christian Beginnings," *Andrews University Seminary Studies* 25 (1987), 163. When McArthur discusses various individual rabbis who seem to have been celibate, he invariably finds a link with ritual purity for the sacrifice which made their celibacy a temporary matter.

[2] *Anagk*, or "distress," seems to have been a technical word which described the sufferings characteristic of the last days (see 1 Thess 3:7; 2 Cor 6:4; 12:10).

[3] Whether the "thorn in the side" of Paul referred to something sexual has been discussed regularly. As early as 1926 Joachim Jeremias surmised that Paul might have been a widower. See his "War Paulus Witwer?," *Zeitschrift NW*, 25 (1926), 310-12 and "Nochmals: War Paulus Witwer?," *Zeitschrift NW*, 28 (1929), 321-23. Against his view see Erich Fascher, "Zur Witwerschaft des Paulus und der Auslegung von 1 Cor 7, 28 (1929), 62-69.

[4] Jerome Murphy-O'Connor, *I Corinthians* (Wilmington, DE: Michael Glazier, 1982), 59.

[5] Dom Jacques Dupont, *Marriage de Divorce dans l'evangile: Matthieu 19, 3-12 et parakles* (Bruges, Belgium: Desclée de Brower, 1959), 161-74. I am indebted to my Capuchin confrere, Michael Fountain, for translating the entire third part of this classic work on eunuchs. Without his help this section would be sorely missing the good scholarship that he has provided for me.

[6] Jerome Murphy-O'Connor, O.P., *What Is Religious Life?: A Critical Reappraisal* (Wilmington, DE: Michael Glazier, 1977), 54.

[7] *Ibid.*

[8] John P. Meier, *Matthew* (Wilmington, DE: Michael Glazier, 1980), 216.

[9] Daniel J. Harrington, S.J., "Matthew," in Dianne Bergant, C.S.A. and Robert J. Karris, eds., *The Collegeville Bible Commentary* (Collegeville, MN: The Liturgical Press, 1988), 889-90.

[10] Pope John Paul II, "Church Committed to Priestly Celibacy," *L'Osservatore Romano*, July 21, 1993. The identification of "church" with the interests of the clergy has been used to sustain the clerical control for centuries.

[11] An early effort to link priestly celibacy with the apostles can be found in 1878 with Gustav Bickell ("Der Zölibat eine apostolische Anordnung," *Zeitschrift für Katholische Theologie* 2 ((1878), 22-64 and "Der Zölibat dennoch eine apostolische Anordnung," *Zeitschrift für Katholische Theologie* 3 (1879), 792-99. In more recent years the argument has been reintroduced by others. See Roman Cholij, *Clerical Celibacy in East and West* (Herefordshire, England: Fowler Wright, 1989), Christian Cochini, *The Apostolic Origins of Priestly Celibacy*, tr. Nelly Mayans (San Francisco: Ignatius Press, 1990), Henri Deen, *Le Celibat des Prêtres dans les Premiers Siécles de l'Eglise* (Paris, 1969), and A. M. Stickler, "Tratti salienti nella storia del celibato," *Sacra Doctina* 15 (1970), 585-620.

[12] "Celibacy Rule Is Reaffirmed by Pope," *The Catholic Herald*, August 4, 1993, 9.

[13] Sandra M. Schneiders, I.H.M., "Women in the First Century and Women in the Contemporary Church," *Biblical Theology Bulletin* 12 (1982), 35.

[14] Henry C. Lea's definitive history of clerical celibacy is *the History of Sacerdotal Celibacy in the Christian Church*. Published in 1867 it reflects an anti-Catholic bias. Yet it is one of the few full-length comprehensive historical surveys of the topic. For a more recent overview, see Paul J. Beaudette, *Ritual Purity in Roman Catholic Priesthood: Using the Work of Mary Douglas to Understand Clerical Celibacy* (Berkeley, CA: Graduate Theological Union, 1994).

[15] See my *The Dysfunctional Church: Addiction and Co-Dependency in the Family of Catholicism* (Notre Dame, IN: Ave Maria, 1991), 79-86 for more on the subject.

[16] Pope Paul VI, "On Priestly Celibacy," June 24, 1967, 1 (Washington, DC: United States Catholic Conference, 1967), 1.

[17] Philip Sheldrake, "Celibacy and Clerical Culture," *The Way Supplement* 77 (1994), 32. Not long after this article was published, Sheldrake, the general editor of *The Way*, left the Jesuits and the priesthood to get married.

[18] Cyprian of Carthage, *Letter* 67:3-4, in *Saint Cyprian Letters* (1-81), trans. Sister Rose Bernard Donna, C.S.J. (Washington, D.C.: Catholic University of America, 1964), 233-35. While grounding ultimate authority in the people, Cyprian also stressed the hierarchical dimension. He insisted on the collegiality of the bishops, within which a unique position of honor was accorded the bishop of Rome. However this honor arose from historical links, not juridical power. Indeed no evidence exists that Rome exploited the Matthew 16 text about Peter's primacy before the middle of the third century.

[19] Beaudette, *Ibid.*, 141-42.

[20] Canon 33, Council of Elvira, in Henricus Denzinger and Adolfus Schonmetzer, S.J., eds. *Enchiridion Symbolorum, Definitionum et Declartionum de Rebus Fidei et Morum*, 119 (Barcinone, Friburgi Gensgoviae, Romae: Herder, 1971), 51. The dating of Elvira recently has been debated. However a greater debate revolves around the text

in question. Tradition had it that Canon 33 arose from the Council of Elvira. This is the position of Cochini, *Ibid.*, 159. However others believe that it was inserted as a canon of the Elvira council much later and actually arise in the late 4th century. See M. Meigne, "Concile ou Collection d'Elire?," *Revue d'Histoire Ecclesiastique* 70 (1975), 361-87.

[21] Pope Siricius, "*Ad Himerium*," 185, in Denzinger-Schonmetzer, 74, 12; also Cochini, *Ibid.*, 5.

[22] Crosby, *Ibid.*, 69-74. See also Charles A. Frazee, "The origins of Clerical Celibacy in the Western Church," *Church History* 41 (1972), 156.

[23] Cochini, *Ibid.*, 5.

[24] Noted in Edward Schillebeeckx, *Celibacy*, tr. C. A. L. Jarrott (New York: Sheed and Ward, 1968), 43.

[25] Peter Brown, *Body and Society: Men, Women, and Sexual Renunciation in Early Christianity* (New York: Columbia University Press, 1988), 142-44.

[26] Beaudette, *Ibid.*, 190.

[27] Peter Damian, "*De Celibatu Sacerdotum*," PL 145.41 Off, in Anne Llewellyn Barstow, "Married Priests and the Reforming Papacy: The Eleventh Century Debates," Texts and Studies in Religion, 12 (New York: Edwin Mellen, 1982), 61.

[28] Ulric, quoted in Barstow, *Ibid.*, 119.

[29] James A. Brudage, *Law, Sex, and Christian Society in Medieval Europe* (Chicago: University of Chicago, 1987), 215.

[30] Bernard J. Cooke, *Ministry to Word and Sacraments: History and Theology* (Philadelphia: Fortress, 1976), 559. See also Beaudette,

Ibid., 264ff.

[31] Barstow, *Ibid.*, 98.

[32] H. Daniel-Rops, *The Protestant Reformation*, tr. Audrey Butler (London: J. M. Dent & Son and New York: E. P. Dutton, 1961), 268.

[33] Canons 9 and 10, council of Trent, in *The Church Teaches: Documents of the Church in English Translation* (St. Louis/London: B. Herder, 1964), 338.

[34] J. D. Crichton, "Church and Ministry from the Council of Trent to the First Vatican Council," in Nicholas Lash and Joseph Rhymer, eds., *The Christian Priesthood* (Denville, NJ: Dimension Books, 1970), 124. I am indebted to Paul Beaudette for directing me to this source.

[35] Beaudette, *Ibid*, 316.

[36] Decree on the Training of Priests," October 28, 1965, no. 10, in Austin Flanner, O.P., gen. Ed., *Vatican Council II: The Conciliar and Post Conciliar Documents* (Collegeville, MN: The Liturgical Press, 1981), 715.

[37] Pope Paul VI, "The Value of the Free and Sovereign Choice of Celibacy," *L'Osservatore Romano*, February 13, 1975, 2.

[38] Heinz-J. Vogels, *Celibacy–Gift or Law? A Critical Investigation* (Kansas City, MO: Sheed & Ward, 1993), 63ff.

[39] *Ibid.*

[40] "Priestly Life and Ministry," 16 in Walter M. Abbott, S.J., gen. ed., *The Documents of Vatican II* (New York: Herder and Herder/Association Press, 1966), 565, 566.

[41] Vogels, *Ibid.*

[42] Canon 277, in James A. Coriden, Thomas J. Green, and Donald E. Heintschel, eds., *The Code of Canon Law: A Test and Commentary* (New York/Mahwah: Paulist, 1985), 209.

[43] Dean R. Hoge, *The Future of Catholic Leadership: Response to the Priest Shortage* (Kansas City: Sheed and Ward, 1987), 144-45.

[44] Karl Rahner, "The Celibacy of the Secular Priest Today," *The Furrow* 19 (1988), 64.

[45] Cardinal Schotte, quoted in David Willey, "Lament of a Vatican-Watcher," *The Tablet* 255 (24 November, 2001), 1658.

[46] Pope John Paul II, Apostolic Letter, "Ordinatio Sacerdotalis," 4, Mary 30, 1994, in *Origins* 24 (1994), 51.

[47] For more on the nature of the binding-degree of the statement, see Francis Sullivan, "New Claims for the Pope," *The Tablet* 248 (1994), 767-769.

[48] "Pope John Paul's Pre-Emptive Strike,"*Ibid.*, 691.

[49] Pope John Paul II, quoting Pope Paul VI, Apostolic Letter, *Ibid.* 1, 49.

[50] *Ibid.*, 2, 51.

[51] "An Overview of the Apostolic Letter," *Origins* 24 (1994), 52.

[52] Cardinal J. Francis Stafford, quoted in Melinda Hennebereger and James Sterngold, "Vatican Meeting on Abuse Issue Is Set to Confront Thorny Subjects," *The New York Times*, April 19, 2002.

[53] John L. Allen, Jr., "Chaotic Vatican Summit Produces Flawed Document," *National Catholic Reporter*, May 10, 2002.

CHAPTER TWO

In What Do We Believe: "One, Holy, Catholic and Apostolic Church"Or One-half, Roman, Curial and Apodictic Clique?

In June, 2003, Frank Keating, former Oklahoma governor and first head of the U.S. Bishops' National Review Board, resigned after comparing some bishops to "La Cosa Nostra," because they continued covering up the extent of clergy molestation. His reference led Cardinal Roger M. Mahony and other bishops, as well as some Board members, to protest. Distinguishing between the church (which, he said, "is not a criminal enterprise") and the bishops, he refused to apologize for his statement, saying: "To resist grand jury subpoenas, to suppress the names of offending clerics, to deny, to obfuscate, to explain away; that is the model of a criminal organization, not my church."[1]

I personally think that Keating went overboard in his reference to the U.S. Bishops as "La Cosa Nostra." However, as this chapter proceeds, especially as we deal with "romanita" in the Roman Curia, one might find the reference somewhat apt, at least for *its* secretive way of operating. And, in the process, one may find quite a few U.S. Bishops agreeing!

The previous chapter's examination of the history related to the imposition of mandatory celibacy showed how forces centered in Rome gradually came to ascendancy over the whole church. The more we know how bishops from around the world—even those of huge dioceses--visiting the Curial offices often do so in fear and intimidation (especially when the offices have received complaints)

37

indicates that, though they may be powerful in their own dioceses, when they get to Rome they become emasculated.

The Curia As An Independent Magisterium

In the dynamics of the Roman Curia as it has come to be constituted and functioning, we find a "parallel magisterium." Its operations now undermine the message and mission of Jesus and the integrity of the Church. Its patterns are undermining the essential identity of the Roman Church as "one, holy, catholic, and apostolic." These authentic signs of the church are being sabotaged by this parallel "one-half (of humanity), Roman, Curial and apodictic" clique (insofar as a "clique" represents an exclusive, closed group of people). It now functions as "the church" with few, if any, voices opposing its unilateral control. In the process, I believe the words that Jesus "said to the crowds and to his disciples" about the religious leaders of his day applies to those of our day in the Roman Church:

> The scribes and the Pharisees sit on Moses' seat; . . . They tie up heavy burdens, hard to bear, and lay them on the shoulders of others; but they themselves are unwilling to lift a finger to move them. . .But you are not to be called rabbi, for you have one teacher, and you are all students. And call no one your father on earth, for you have one Father–the one in heaven. Nor are you to be called instructors, for you have one instructor, the Messiah. The greatest among you will be your servant. All who exalt themselves will be humbled, and all who humble themselves will be exalted (Mt. 23:1-12).

I'm sure that, at the time of Jesus, as now, there were many religious leaders who, individually, were fine men. Yet, then, as now, their voices were silenced by the critical mass that constituted the leadership group to which they belonged. Indeed today, the very Church whose foundations we Catholics trace to Jesus Christ has become constellated around and controlled by one group of religious leaders whose hardness of heart evidence the vary arrogance of power that Jesus condemned. It is their collective abuse of power that has been unmasked as we learn of individual cases of priestly sexual abuse here and abroad.

In examining the decrees of the Second Vatican Council, I find but one mention of the Curia. The Decree on the Pastoral Office of Bishops states: "In exercising his supreme, full and immediate authority over the universal Church the Roman Pontiff employs the various departments of the Roman Curia, which act in his name and by his authority for the good of the churches and in the service of the sacred pastors."[2] The Curia's role is further detailed in Canon Law: "The Supreme Pontiff usually conducts the business of the universal Church by means of the Roman Curia."[3] Thus, whether conciliarly or canonically, we cannot question the right and even the need for the Curia to do "the business of the universal church." That pertains to the Pope. However I do have questions when the well-being of the whole church is jeopardized by the actions of such few men.

That Pope John Paul II himself seemed to recognize problems with the Curia appears evident in his 1995 encyclical *Ut Unum Sint*, "That They May Be One." At a press briefing announcing this letter on ecumenism, Cardinal Edward Cassidy, president of the Pontifical Council for Promoting Christian Unity, told the journalists: "The pope sees the Catholic position on the primacy as an essential point of faith, but the way it is exercised is a question to be discussed."[4] Much of the encyclical involved a call for dialogue.

Building on this call for dialogue, retired Archbishop of San Francisco, John Quinn gave a talk at Oxford entitled "Considering the Papacy." In it he spent much time discussing the Curia as an obstacle to ecumenism. He distinguished between the substance or canonical status of the Curia and its style.[5] He referred to the church's structure in a threefold way: the Pope, the Curia and the episcopate. He said: "This makes it possible for the Curia to see itself as exercising oversight and authority over the College of Bishops, to see itself as subordinate to the pope but superior to the College of Bishops. To the degree that this is so and is reflected in the policies and actions of the Curia it obscures and diminishes both the doctrine and the reality of episcopal collegiality."[6]

While many praised Archbishop Quinn for speaking his mind on the matter (even if he did so only after his retirement), I find his comments about the tripartite idea of "the church" lacking the theological notion of the role of the faithful via the "*sensus fidelium.*"[7] He also makes no mention of theological teaching regarding what the community of faith believes. However, arguing with Archbishop Quinn is not my purpose here. I merely want to show that this "*tertium quid*" or "third entity," the name given by the Archbishop to describe the Roman Curia, has overextended its mandate as the sole guarantor, much less the exclusive interpreter, of what it means to be "one, holy, catholic, and apostolic."

While Archbishop Quinn's remarks made the news when he first uttered them, I much prefer the approach of Rembert Weakland, former Archbishop in Milwaukee. He highlighted "two different and competing perspectives on how to view the church and its functioning." One "talks more about the collegial role of bishops, the *sensus fidelium* or the insights of the faithful, and the role of the Spirit as animating the whole body of Christ." The other is what he calls "ultramontanism."[8]

It "postulates a highly centralized Church, a striving for more uniformity and conformity." He notes: "The extreme temptation for the ultamontanist is to reduce all teaching authority in the Church to papal teaching only. They see the papal magisterium as all that really matters. The role of the bishop is reduced to implementing orders received."[9] Such a view stands contrary to the Second Vatican Council and the encyclical, both of which reject the notion of bishops serving as mere "vicars of the Roman Pontiff."[10] While the Pope has primacy, that primacy is exercised within the collegiality of all the bishops and never outside the *sensus fidelium.*

Increasingly the Curia undermines the power of the bishops, especially when they act collegially at regional or national levels. In the process it also denigrates the integrity of the papal office and the inherent truth found in the *sensus fidelium.* While it purports to act in the name of the pope, it actually has come to function as a kind of church-unto-itself, answerable to no one except, perhaps, the pope. In the process it threatens not only the authentic hierarchical dimension of the church which I call "the church of Matthew 16" but the rank-and-file faithful, whom I call "the church of Matthew 18."[11] The consequence of this can be described as the disease I noted in the Introduction that saps the entire body's strength.

The consequent pathology that has come to infect the institutional family can be considered a kind of "creeping Curialism" or "malignant magisterialism."[12] The result is that bishops watch with sadness as it invades the hierarchy, people trying to challenge it live in fear of its unilateral power and other ecclesial bodies want nothing to do with the rest of us as long as their behavior goes unchecked and the Body of Christ suffers serious damage.

I don't want to go overboard using the metaphor of disease in treating the Curia. As the administrative arm of the Pope, the Roman Curia often serves a valuable function. It's just that what I call the Curia's "shadow side" too often casts a pall over the positive things that may be done by its various office(r)s. But, as long as denial and delusion about its corrupting dynamics are *de rigueur*, its autocratic rulings will continue to erode the faith of many in "the church." Especially when it has become "the church," it becomes important to discover how its dynamics have created the malaise that exists when people consider the flaws of "the church."

The Roman Curia revolves around the Secretariat of State, nine Congregations, three Tribunals and eleven Pontifical Councils. Its main functions operate through the Congregations, especially six of the nine: the Congregation for the Doctrine of the Faith (once called "The Holy Office"), the Congregations for Bishops, Clergy, and Catholic Education (which includes Seminaries), the Congregation for Divine Worship and the Sacraments and the Congregation for Institutes of Consecrated Life and for Societies of Apostolic Life (CICLSAL). In theory the Secretariat of State, the Congregations, the Councils and the three Tribunals have "equal juridical status." Yet, as in so many other matters, some seem "more equal than others." We find this, for instance, with Cardinal Joseph Ratzinger. He chairs the Congregation on the Doctrine of the Faith (CDF). It exists "to promote and safeguard the doctrine of faith and morals in the whole Catholic world; therefore, those things belong to it which touch this matter in any way." It alone has authority to decide what things belong to it–which can be anything it decides. He also chairs other Commissions: the International Theological Commission and the Pontifical Biblical Commission. This enables him to control the interpretation of the two sources that constitute the identity of our Church: scripture and tradition. In effect, this one Curial Cardinal controls what we believe. Thus, the question of this chapter: "In What Do We Believe."

In 381 at Constantinople, the church's marks were defined as "one, holy, catholic and apostolic." They are common to the creed of Christian churches in both the East and the West, among the "Orthodox" and "Uniates," "Catholics" and "Protestants." All mainline churches end the Nicene Creed the same way: "We believe in one holy catholic and apostolic Church." These characteristic "marks of the church" have been a subject for ecumenical dialogues for quite some time. Unfortunately, in the church called "Roman Catholic," an interpretation of scripture and the development of tradition have led to these universal marks taking on a different flavor.

In his encyclical on ecumenism, *Ut Unum Sint*, Pope John Paul II refers to the four marks of the church,[13] but, we have seen, the Curia hardly gets a mention. Nonetheless the Curia has become one of the biggest obstacles to seeking unity among the churches and, with the revelations about clerical abuse of minors (often same-sex) in this country and of women, including nuns, in developing nations, we need to examine what has gone wrong about these traditional "marks of the church." This brings me to ask, regarding the first "mark" of the church:

Is Our's "One" Church or "One-Half" Church Because of the Control of a Patriarchal Clique?

Division is nothing new in the church. We know that the very night the Fourth Gospel says Jesus prayed for unity among them, his followers were scattered all over the place. Consequently we shouldn't be surprised that the scattering still continues. Despite the fact that various divisions may have characterized the community of disciples from the beginning, unity or "oneness" is the first mark of the church if it is authentic to its calling.

When Paul talked about the church being "one body" (1 Cor. 12:12f) and said there was "one Lord, one faith, one baptism" (Eph. 4:5), it was centuries before the split between Eastern and Western "churches" (1054) and a millennium before the Protestant Reformation (1517). In those days, despite differences, basic uniformity in creed, cult and culture obtained. However, since 1054 the Romans and Orthodox are in schism[14] and since 1517 all sorts of Protestant denominations and sects have arisen among ecclesial communities, to say nothing of the divisions and polarities among us Catholics.

I believe the source for most of our problems around unity or oneness arises when we stress our tradition before our scriptural links. If your ultimate starting point on unity begins with Tradition as we know it today, even if it highlights the Second Vatican Council, instead of the Scriptures, you are showing your bias regarding one of the two fonts of revelation. The not-so-subtle message remains: the institutional expression of Catholicism identified with "Tradition" takes precedence over the person and message of Jesus Christ found in the "Scriptures." I know that Pope John Paul II has given primacy to the scriptures in his speeches and in the encyclical as well. But because he places such emphasis on the "authentic teaching office" as having "a special role in the explanation and proclamation of the written word of God," when that teaching office has often been historically identified with Curial abuses, problems in ecumenism can result.

While "oneness" is a mark of the true church, a contrasting kind of oneness marks this other Curial group which thinks of itself as *the* church. Yet, because the Curia is almost exclusively male, with every one of its heads being male, it represents only one-half of the church. Its decisions represent only a male perspective (and therefore only half of the human viewpoint). This half-of-the-whole is characterized by a kind of rigid uniformity often enforced unilaterally as well as by a single-mindedness bordering on ideology that expresses itself in autocratic and unaccountable ways. It is reflected in the "centralizing tendency" that the late Cardinal Basil Hume of England warned as undermining subsidiarity or decisions made collegially at the local level. An example of this can be found in the way Cardinal Ratzinger told bishops' conferences that they could not ordain alcoholics and celiacs (those allergic to the gluten in wheat) because of "the centrality of the celebration of the Eucharist in the life of the priest"--as though wheat can be the only "fruit of the earth and the work of human hands" that the God of all creation finds acceptable for the sacrifice.[15]

I find it quite paradoxical that the Pope can write a whole encyclical and talk about unity that can be achieved only by dialogue with those outside Catholicism, while his administrative arm, the Curia, consistently refuses dialogue within the body of Christ called church. This call for dialogue is what Archbishop Quinn appealed to when he raised questions about the Curia. However, almost immediately his request was attacked by the late Cardinal John O'Connor of New York. Cardinal O'Connor was one of the U.S. Cardinals known for his unquestioning fealty to the Roman Curia. He insisted that the encyclical doesn't envision dialogue among those inside the Roman church, only those outside. However, the strength of a truth is as good as its universal application. Hence, in my view, I believe this is one of those occasions when the Pope's words on dialogue should be equally applied within as well as without.

The Pope calls such dialogue an occasion for "an examination of conscience" that will lead to conversion. He declares: "Christian unity is possible, provided that we are humbly conscious of having sinned against unity and are convinced of our need for conversion. Not only personal sins must be forgiven and left behind, but also social sins, which is to say the sinful 'structures' themselves which have contributed and can still contribute to division and to the reinforcing of division."[16] Some of us would say the pope should apply to his own Curia this principle and work for its reform or structural conversion, granted the divisions we have between women and men, cleric and lay, gay and straight, the bishops and the Curia, and, increasingly, among the bishops themselves.

In the early 90s, when the U.S. Bishops' Conference (USCCB) was able to reach some kind of agreement on a pastoral letter on women, it was scuttled due, in good part, to the intervention of the CDF.[17] This is one reason why a group of U.S. bishops called for a restructuring of the Bishops Conference that stresses more dialogue among the bishops and between the bishops and the Curia[18] and why, at the international level, another group of bishops called for another ecumenical council to restructure the Roman Church. Next you read about one bishop excommunicating members of the church reform group called Call to Action and other bishops publicly admitting they belonged to CTA. Meanwhile Cardinal Ratzinger declares, in effect, that those agreeing with CTA's position that women should be priests are "outside" the faith of the church!

In preparing this chapter, I examined my files to discover how many times I wrote to the heads of Curia offices--from the Papal Nuncio in Washington, to Cardinal Ratzinger, to the head of the Congregation of Bishops, to the head of the Congregation that oversees my own Order's relations with the Vatican. I counted at least a half-dozen letters. In only one instance did I receive a response. While I cannot call his response "dialogical," it was a response.

I had written a letter after the CICLSAL had refused our Province's request to have a lay-brother be our Vicar Provincial. The Province had elected him to this Office. However, because we were defined by Canon Law as a "clerical" order, he needed a dispensation to be a major superior. So I wrote to the late Cardinal Hamer of CICLSAL arguing for his case. At the conclusion I added: "As we always receive a reply from our civil authorities when we register our concerns, I would hope I might expect the same from you as my canonical authority. The last time I wrote you I never got a response."

This time I got a response. I received the next month Protocol number 13234/87 on the letterhead of the "*Congregatio pro Religiosis et Institutis Saecularibus.*" Dated "Rome, April 8, 1988," it contained three paragraphs. The first two had one sentence and the last had two. It read:

Dear Father Crosby,

I have received your letter of March 4th concerning Brother David Schwab.

Thank you for taking the time to write and present your opinion on the question of "the equality of all the men in solemn vows."

May God continue to bless you and all the members of your community. Let us pray for each other.

Sincerely in Christ

s/f. Jerome Card. Hamer, O.P.

The Cardinal referred to my thoughts as an "opinion." This reflects a Roman ranking around differences related to doctrine and discipline: the laity has opinions and theologians have "considered opinions;" the Curia possesses the "truth." Anyone speaking "outside" its truth, it considers outside the faith of the church. This approach to truth reflects the ideology operating at all levels, despite the fact that Pope John Paul II stated in his January 1, 2002 New Year's letter that no one person or group possess the whole truth.

In his encyclical, the Pope elaborates in a whole section on "Dialogue as Means of Resolving Disagreements." His points are profound. He writes: "There must be charity toward one's partner in dialogue, and humility with regard to the truth which comes to light and which might require a review of assertions and attitudes."[19] That we have a Curia unwilling to dialogue is not only disappointing. Using John Paul II's own words, it represents a counter-sign to the authenticity of "unity" as a sign of the true church.

When we witness decrees instead of dialogue and one-way dictates instead of genuine discussion, differences are not settled; they are merely repressed or suppressed. And when fear instead of fidelity characterizes peoples' response to such decrees we are in a situation characterized by Curial coercion and control rather than genuine care. Any clinical or social psychologist would say such dynamics reflect relationships defined by abuse.[20] It's in this sense I move to the second of the "marks" and ask:

Is Our Church "Holy" or "Roman"?

In our living room in Milwaukee, where we brothers also pray, we have an icon of Archbishop Oscar Romero, the priest who was killed while celebrating Mass in San Salvador. "Why isn't he canonized yet?," someone asked one day as she prayed with us. Somebody else replied: "He wasn't Mother Theresa of Calcutta. He threatened the Curia." Despite dying a martyr's death "Rome" has not moved with dispatch to consider his holiness seriously.

The Document on the Church (*Lumen Gentium*) states: "The Church, whose mystery is set forth by this sacred Council, is held, as a matter of faith, to be unfailingly holy." The more original version says it is "indefectibly holy."[21] This is not because of anything it manifests in itself, but because of the self-donation of Christ who gave himself to her as his bride in order to make her holy through the power of his Spirit. This holiness, the next Chapter declares, is "real but imperfect."[22] How real it is and how imperfect it can be is realized when we turn to the sixth chapter of Isaiah. It describes the prophet's image of holiness. In Isaiah we find that holiness is godliness.

When Isaiah talks about the Seraphim and their proclamation around the throne of God about God being "holy, holy, holy," from this vision of God he became acutely aware of his own unholiness as well as that of the world around him, including those people who were the religious leaders. In a parallel way, I believe, the closer we come to understand God's holiness and immensity, we come to see how unholy and petty some of the Curia's thinking can be when, for instance, it tells us this God (who alone is holy and among whose persons there is no inequality) wills discrimination against women at the highest level of the church.

Jesus chose these same words from Isaiah about God's holiness and the unholiness of the priestly system and applied them to the situation of the religious leaders of his day. However, the fact that the leaders of Isaiah's religious institution would not even listen to a prophet from God leads me from the second sign of an authentic church to its opposite notion. In the case of the Curia, I call this counter-sign *"romanita."*

In describing "romanita" *The Catholic Fact Book* says: "It is attached as a rule to clergy of whatever rank who are stationed in Rome, dependent on Rome for position and favor, or aspiring to same in or of Rome."[23] "Romanita" represents a clerical ideology that has made its adherents blind and deaf lest there be a change of heart. I find it alive and well in much of the Curia.

While romanita might refer to those "in or of Rome," its reach is global. Romanita's style became evident to all in the English-speaking world who observed the way the Congregation for the Doctrine of Faith handled the issue of inclusive language in the *New Catechism of the Catholic Church,* the Lectionary and Sacramentary, as well as the General Instruction for the Roman Missal. The U.S. Bishops approved for liturgical use the more-inclusive language of the New Revised Standard Version (NRSV [1991]). Their approval was confirmed the next year by the Congregation for Worship and Sacraments. Yet the confirmation was *rescinded* by the Congregation of the Doctrine of the Faith in 1994. Not only did the CDF override another Curial Congregation, it negated the decision of an episcopal conference. As the head of the Congregation which originally approved the translation said, "From the moment in which the doctrinal congregation makes a statement, we cannot act differently."[24] So much for being "more or less equal." The result? As one liturgist said of these dynamics: "we're being micro-managed by the Curia."

This case makes it clear that the issue is not about changing the English language. Rather it shows how the reality represented in romanita must be preserved, even if it alienates the majority of a continent. Romanita must remain the official language or articulation of all local churches, according to the Curia. So the CDF's decision has little or nothing to do with Australian, Canadian, British, Indian, Irish, New Zealand or U.S. English. It has much more to do with the preservation of "male" as the official *leitmotif* of the Roman, Curial church.

The Chairman of the U.S. Bishops' Ad Hoc Committee for the Review of Scripture Translations is Auxiliary Bishop Richard Sklba of Milwaukee. He noted publicly that the Curia's decision was "pastorally and ecumenically confusing." He said:

> Most people in our country do want a liturgical text which is inclusive in the language. To the extent the issue hinges on that, it matters. Then it matters because the pastoral authority of American bishops could seem to be at stake. We bishops may be divided on strategies, we may disagree, but we bishops have a sense of our responsibility for the faith of this nation, and the people in the pews expect that. They do not expect that some group of people outside of this nation would have such extensive authority within our culture. It's very undermining. And the person in the pew could also see this as undermining the legitimacy of biblical scholarship.[25]

While the U.S. bishops made no significant corporate public protest or questioned the Curia's de-facto undermining of their authority as pastors, the Canadian bishops seemed less codependent. They challenged the decision, not so much on theological or ideological grounds, but financial ones. The majority of their Novalis Lectionary already had been printed; it had to be used. On November 9, 1994 the CDF blinked toward Canada. But its eyes remain closed to the U.S. And our bishops shut their mouths without evident protest.[26] Later the Canadian bishops also were told to make revisions for Curial approval.

Another way the Curia intervened in the U.S. Bishops' work relates to efforts by the Roman Curia to take over the fourth draft of the Bishops' Pastoral on Women. The head of the six-bishop committee during the nine year effort was Bishop Joseph Imesch of Joliet. He declared that dealing with the Curia during this time was "like going to the dentist."[27] The Bishops' own National Advisory Council had said the Curia-influenced draft was "defensive and authoritarian rather than pastoral."[28] Despite warnings from some U.S. bishops that a rejection of the Cardinal Ratzinger-reinforced fourth rendition might be seen as disloyalty to the magisterium, its approval was rejected.[29] The result was a 1992 document on Domestic Violence that was slightly revised in 2002. As we'll see in chapter six, its findings say equally as much about Ecclesiastical Violence.

If "Beltway Fever" refers to the disease suffered by people overly-identified with Washington in a way that isolates them from mainstream citizens, "romanita" does the same to those suffering from it vis-à-vis many in the pews. As with the "Beltway" bureaucrats, their world is the real world. It's the classic example of "*Roma locuta, causa finita*"--Rome has spoken, the matter is ended." Isn't its mentality evident in the response of Cardinal Ratzinger on the issue of women's ordination? Because we have said so, there will be no more talk, much less dialogue, about it. As if there *ever* was!

The Curia's main representative in the United States resides within the Beltway, in Washington DC. Some years ago, when the Conference of Major Superiors of Men held their annual meeting in Washington, out of courtesy, they invited the Apostolic Delegate to address their gathering. I've never seen so many church leaders visibly upset. I was amazed at the responses of the Provincials toward the talk. "He talked down to us," said one. Another declared, "He talked to us like he really didn't care whether we listened or not. It was as though he was saying, 'I'm the Nuncio and you're not and I'll say what I want.' Nothing you say will affect my position. He didn't even seem prepared." Another superior with more men in his jurisdiction than some bishops said, "I was insulted. And I was ashamed of us because we just sat there and nobody challenged him."

The Curia has been around a long time. In its present model it was founded formally by Pope Sixtus V in 1588. From its earlier version in the time of Adrian VI (1522-1523) until John Paul II, not only all popes but their Curial extension were dominated by Italians. Even when efforts have been made to "reform" it--as early as Nicholas of Cusa (1401-1464) none seem to have created the desired transformation, including the latest effort that took place not all that long ago.[30] However, while it changed the Curial structure, it was not a structural change. And so it goes today. We hear Pope John Paul II in *Ut Unum Sint* declare:

> In the teaching of the Second Vatican Council there is a clear connection between renewal, conversion and reform. The

council states that "Christ summons the church, as she goes her pilgrim way, to that continual reformation of which she always has need, insofar as she is an institution of human beings here on earth. Therefore, if the influence of events or of the times has led to deficiencies. . . these should be appropriately rectified at the proper moment."[31]

"No Christian community can exempt itself from this call," he immediately concludes. Unfortunately, too often from practice, we can immediately conclude as well: "No Christian community, except the Roman Curia, can exempt itself from this call." This thought leads us to ask, in light of the third "mark" of an authentic church:

Is Our Church "Catholic/Universal" or "Curial/Clerical"?

During a highpoint in the second wave of pedophilia, I presided at a home baptism at my cousins'. Their great uncle and aunt and great grandmother are Lutherans. During the ceremony I found myself choking back the word "catholic" when I led the Nicene Creed. Why? I think it has more to do more with how "catholic" has been identified with its Curial characteristic and "*romanita*" (as well as its aberrations in pedophilia) than what is authentically catholic.

The Greek adjective *katholikos* comes from two words: *kath* and *holou* they mean "according to the whole." Basically the word means "whole" or "universal." The first known use of the term comes from St. Ignatius of Antioch. He wrote the church at Smyrna: ". . . where Jesus Christ is, there is the catholic church."[32]

The Second Vatican Council says the Church's catholicity can be found in four main areas: the Blessed Trinity as its source, its presence among all races, nations and cultures, its rich diversity and its encounter with all humanity.[33] However, if we just consider how the Trinity is reflected in catholicity I think we're going to find another "god" if our church's "trinity" mirrors the centralized, male, Roman Curia. If "catholic" means trinitarian, it is open; however, all-too-often Curia seems equated with being closed. If we understand the Trinity as a community of persons who are equal and remain equal only when they related to each other in a way that ensures each other having full access to the group's resources, we find a structural obstacle to this trinitarian grounding of all reality in the Congregation of Faith's insistence that only men can have full access to all the church's sacramental resources, including ordination.

When Cardinal Ratzinger issued his statement saying the non-ordination of women was "definitive" insofar as it reflected the will of [the triune] God and that those who did not subscribe to it were outside the Catholic Church, it became clear to me he was not talking about the "catholic" church that is inclusive, as is the trinity, but his "Curial" church that is sexist. Yet, because my book on *Celibacy* was about to be published[34] in which I disagreed with the papal teaching on women, for my integrity, I wrote him the following letter:

Most Reverend and Dear Cardinal Ratzinger:

This is the first time I have written to you. [It really wasn't; I also had written earlier to support the inclusive translations of the scriptures and the sacramentary, but he didn't answer, so I forgot]. I do so in light of the CDF's November 18, 1995 declaration re: Pope John Paul II's statement on the non-ordination of women. I find it illogical, inconsistent and ill-conceived to argue that because Jesus didn't choose women to be his apostles that anyone can thus conclude that, in that given milieu, he *intended* this in a way *to exclude* them from full leadership in the future. Also, to argue that such a "non-choice" represents not only the will of the Jesus of history but of the Christ of our faith in whom there is neither male nor female appears to me even less convincing. Finally, somehow to make a conclusion that this is the actual will of our God (in whom there is no exclusiveness) is beyond my comprehension. . .

I heard you supported the 18 Nov. statement only to keep greater harm from coming to our Church if an actual "infallible" declaration would have been made by our Pope. If so, thank you for your finesse. But if you do agree with it, I ask you to consider the integrity of many of us loyal Catholics who can no longer fathom making such a statement, much less the "rationale" used to support it. I would be pleased if you decide to share this letter with His Holiness. And if you would care to dialogue with me on these reflections or others related to it that I have shared in my public writings, I would invite it.

He never responded. This makes me ask: If "catholic" means open and public, why does "Curial" often mean closed and secret? An example can be found in the behind-the-scenes way the Congregation for Catholic Education moved to keep certain Jesuits from leadership at different pontifical schools and institutions of higher learning, one of them my own former spiritual director.[35] For many years we watched the maneuvering regarding the efforts of the U.S. bishops to keep the Curia's vision of "Catholic Education" from defining Catholic education in the U.S.A. Again the Vatican prevailed with nary a dissenting voice among the U.S. bishops. At the time of this writing, however, there seems to have been little episcopal action on *Ex Corde Ecclesiae* ("From the Heart of the Church").

In country after country, Catholic bishops are emasculated by the Curia—all in the name of orthodoxy. Frank Morrisey, OMI, one of the most respected canon lawyers in Canada notes that the 70 members of the Canadian Conference of Catholic Bishops, with one or two exceptions, have lost their authority. Whereas the CCCB was once one of the most progressive conferences in the Church, he explains: "The bishops are no longer proactive. Everything is centralized at the level of the Holy See and for all practical purposes, it's the Holy See that determines the agenda."[36]

Orthodoxy is critical for all authentic teaching; however when the true sign of "orthodoxy" seems an uncritical acceptance of statements that beg for further clarification and nuance in the name of apostolic office, one can ask:

Is Our Church "Apostolic" or "Apodictic"?

The discussion around apostolicity as a sign of the true church, too often in some Roman Catholic circles, has been overly-identified with the simplistic issue of "apostolic succession:" namely the fact that one validly consecrated bishop was consecrated by another validly consecrated bishop, back to the apostles (who never were ordained as we know it today). If we consider how bishops are chosen for this consecration, we find Curial control all over. A pattern seems to have emerged that easily discounts the guidance of bishops in a provincial district. As one bishop said quite simply, "Recommendations of (arch)bishops in the Province are not listened to." For his part, Archbishop Quinn has noted that:

> it is not uncommon for bishops of a province to discover that no candidate they proposed has been accepted for approval. On the other hand, it may happen that candidates whom bishops do not approve at all may be appointed. . . . Under the existing policy, collegiality in the appointment of bishops consists largely in offering bishops an opportunity to make suggestions. But the real decisions are made at other levels [of the Curia]: the nuncio, the Congregation of Bishops, the Secretariat of State.[37]

Even for Archbishop Quinn, that the laity should be involved is not even on the "radar screen." The Roman Curia's attitude of knowing better than people at the local level is not limited only to the Secretariat of State, the Congregation of Bishops and the nunciatures in capital cities who now seem to be defining who will go where as local bishops. It has affected many of us in religious congregations as well.

Closer to home, my own community of Capuchins has experienced its heavy hand. I've already noted the response of CICLSAL to my Province's request that a lay-brother be allowed to be our Vicar Provincial. Its refusal was extended again in 2002 when we elected a non-ordained brother to be our highest superior (minister provincial). The Curia's curious ways become even "curiouser" when we consider its response to my Order's request that we be considered a community of equals having all offices in the Order open to all of us perpetually professed brothers.

Having met countless times with members of the Curia, our General Definitory would not capitulate to its demands that we put into our Constitutions that we are a clerical order. Having exhausted all avenues, we finally appealed to the Holy Father himself.

Not long after our appeal, the Order received a reply from CICLSAL that its request had been considered, but that it was now the decision of the "Holy See" that the clerics-only clause be put into the legislation. However, since the Capuchins had a Polish council-member who knew a Polish secretary of the pope, he asked him if the pope actually had considered the Capuchin's appeal. When he said the pope was unaware of the appeal, the Order made a formal appeal to the pope.

In other words, by saying, it "was 'the will of the Holy See' that you put into your constitutions that you are a clerical order," it would lead us to think this meant the Holy Father had so willed it. This makes any thinking person ask: Were CICLSAL's devious ways with us just an isolated incident? Was this really an exception to its rule of even-handedness? It's hard to believe so. Because of the secrecy we'll not likely ever know the face behind the action, much less the name beneath the face. In this case the Holy See is not the Holy Father, but some Curial official who is less interested in promoting truth than another agenda. It doesn't seem to matter that, if it would have happened, this would have reinforced the Curia, but undermined the Capuchin charism, and thus, compromised the integrity of the church. When such dynamics might characterize this "Holy See," we need to be very careful.

More and more, theologians are not limiting the notion of apostolicity to succession through episcopal consecration, but going deeper, to the evangelical notion of the church being apostolic in the sense of all baptized people being entrusted with the mission of Jesus to go into the whole world as priest, prophet and ruler; to be proclaimer, healer and teacher. Sad to say, however, many forces in the Curia seem more intent on limiting that apostolicity to their interpretation of what authentic teaching in our ecclesial community might be. In this sense it too-often seems they are more preoccupied with orthodoxy than orthopraxy, with deciding doctrine than preaching pastorally. In the process the very purpose of the apostolic office itself gets compromised.

I believe an example of this can be found when the CDF usurped the jurisdiction of CICLSAL over Father Robert Nugent and

Sister Jeannine Gramick, as well as those U.S. bishops who promoted pastoral care to homosexual persons through an "outstretched hand." Instead, I believe, they gave the back of their hand to Robert and Jeannine. At the same time the CDF seems to have violated church teaching (Synod of Bishops, 1971) about dialogue and the right of those accused to know their accusers. This brings me to my final point about the Curial church as being apodictic.

Webster's New Twentieth Century Dictionary defines "apodictic" as something or someone that is "absolutely certain; evident beyond contradiction."[38] Apodicticness and "romanita" are poles that, too often, seem to define the parameters of patriarchal control that exercises its God-given power autocratically rather than apostolically.

As I consider this attitude of absolute certainty I am reminded of the notion of a "parallel magisterium" that I have alluded to earlier. As far as I know, the image was first used in The Puebla Document that came from the second large gathering of Latin American bishops in 1978. It referred to the *iglesia popular* or "church of the people." They feared these might become independent of the bishops. They quoted Pope John Paul II as saying such a view could well be inspired by "familiar ideological forms of conditioning."[39]

Since Puebla the Curial forces have been able to decimate the "popular church;" however these same forces are alive and very much a "parallel magisteria" answerable, it seems, to no one. Thus, it seems to me that the "familiar ideological forms of conditioning" that characterize what John Paul II years later noted in Nicaragua about what he called the "parallel magisteria" there[40] fit what I have been trying to say about the one-half, Roman, Curial and apodictic structure operating, not in Nicaragua but throughout the church, as a "*tertium quid*," a third force. Too often this parallel magisterium operates with impunity. It is unanswerable to the bishops, much less the people, and often seems unaccountable even to the Pope (if our experience as Capuchins serves as a model). This needs to be challenged if unity outside and inside our church is to be realized. The challenge must be made if authority is to be exercised in a manner that won't incur the some condemnatory response from Jesus today that he noted in the passage mentioned at the beginning of this chapter.

I'm struck by Bishop Donald Trautman's comments which he made to priests in 1998 regarding power in the church, even though he too limits it among the apostolic group: "Those with the charism of authority must always be mindful of the primacy of Peter and show proper obedience and respect. But they also need to ponder the Epistle to the Galatians where it shows Paul protesting to Peter. Such a protest is not only biblical and historical, it is also justified and, in some circumstances, a sacred duty for the good of the Church."[41]

With Bishop Trautman's caution, I conclude this chapter. As I do, I think of the scripture passage that follows upon Jesus declaring how he was going to build *his church*. He promises Peter the keys of heaven and the power to bind and loose (Mt. 16:17-19), the latter, we will see in chapter six, he also has given the community (Mt. 18:16-18). It happened upon Jesus declaring "he must go to Jerusalem and undergo great suffering at the hands of the elders and chief priests and scribes, and be killed, and on the third day be raised" (Mt. 16:21). In response, Peter utters his first infallible statement after being named "blessed." To make it even more infallible, he even invokes God in his declaration of absolute certitude: "God forbid it, Lord! This must never happen to you" (Mt. 16:22). I often say this was Peter's first infallible statement (i.e., "it must never. . ."); yet it was wrong. As such, it incurred Jesus' rejection.

Jesus' response to Peter should remind all of us--Pope and Bishops, Curia and Concerned Catholics, that there is only one ultimate source of all authority in the church, namely Jesus himself: "Get behind me, Satan! You are a stumbling block to me."[42] Continually all of us, but in a special way, given my remarks here, the Curia which has covered itself in the mantle of Peter, need to hear Jesus' reminder again: "You are setting your mind not on divine things but on human things" (Mt. 16:23). I believe the Curia too often has shown itself to be all too often a very human entity. In the process it has placed heavy burdens on others' shoulders. It's up to us who are the church to continue to try to lift them off.

One of these burdens is celibacy. In the next chapters I will show the inconsistencies involved when it has become embedded, enculturated and mandated as the only way its leaders will be able to function. I will then show the toll it takes on many clerics as well.

Chapter Notes

[1] Frank Keating, quoted in Daniel J. Wakin, "Refusing to Recant, Keating Resigns as Church Panel Chief," *The New York Times*, June 17, 2003.

[2] Decree on the Pastoral Office of Bishops in the Church ("*Christus Dominus*"), 9, in Austin Flannery, O.P., *Vatican II: The Conciliar and Post Conciliar Documents* (Collegeville, MN: The Liturgical Press, 1980), 568.

[3] The two pertinent canons declare: (360) The Supreme Pontiff usually conducts the business of the universal Church by means of the Roman Curia, which fulfills its duty in his name and by his authority for the good and the service of the churches; it consists of the Secretariat of State or the Papal Secretariat, the Council for the Public Affairs of the Church, congregations, tribunals and other institutions, whose structure and competency are defined in special law. (361) In this Code the term "Apostolic See" or "Holy See" applies not only to the Roman Pontiff but also to the Secretariat of State, the Council for the Public Affairs of the church and other institutions of the Roman Curia, unless the nature of the matter or the context of the words makes the contrary evident. *Code of Canon Law: Latin-English Edition* (Washington, DC: Canon Law Society of America, 1983), 131.

[4] Cardinal Edward Cassidy, quoted in Fr. Richard McBrien, Essays in Dialogue, "How Papacy Is Exercised Remains Crucial Issue," [Milwaukee] *Catholic Herald*, June 22, 1995.

[5] Archbishop John R. Quinn, "Considering the Papacy," *Origins* (1996), 120.

[6] Quinn, *Ibid.*, V, 122.

[7] Pope John Paul II, in his encyclical *Ut Unum Sint* itself, seems to acknowledge the role of the *sensus fidelium* when he writes: "We are in fact dealing with issues which frequently are matters of faith, and these require universal consent, extending from the bishops to the lay faithful, all of whom have received the anointing of the Holy Spirit. It is the same Spirit who assists the magisterium and awakens the *sensus fidei.*" No. 80, *Origins* 25 (1995), 67. For a good, understandable interpretation of this notion, see Avery Dulles, "Sensus Fidelium," *America* 155 (1986), 240-142, 263. It seems the need for more attention to the sensus fidelium is also a point raised by the group of bishops seeking more dialogue among the bishops and between the bishops and the Vatican. See Smith, *Ibid.*, and "40 Bishops Say Church Needs Way to Dialogue with Rome," *National Catholic Reporter*, June 30, 1995, 3.

[8] For more on the "ultramontanist" tendencies of American Catholicism, see Patricia Byrne, C.S.J., "American Ultramontanism," *Theological Studies* 56 (1995), 301-326.

[9] Archbishop Rembert G. Weakland, O.S.B., Herald of Hope Weekly Column: "Differences in the Church," December 28, 1995, *Catholic Herald*, 3.

[10] Dogmatic Constitution on the Church (*"Lumen Gentium"*), 27, in Flannery, *Ibid.*, 383.

[11] Michael H. Crosby, *The Dysfunctional Church: Addiction and Codependency in the Family of Catholicism* (Notre Dame: Ave Maria, 1991). The difference in the two churches will be discussed in chapter six.

[12] In a fine piece that can serve as an elaboration on my comments here, Richard A. McCormick refers to "creeping infallibility" ad "magisterial maximalism." See "The Chill Factor: Recent Roman Interventions," *America* 150 (1990), 476.

[13] *Ut Unum Sint*, 94, *Ibid.*, 69.

[14] The reality of the East-West schism was apparent when Aleksy II, the Patriarch of the Russian Orthodox Church, did not agree to meet with Pope John Paul II. Celestine Bohlen, "Pope Arrives in Hungary To an Ecumenical Letdown," *The New York Times,* September 7, 1996, 6.

[15] Ingrid Shafer, "Real Presence a Function of Gluten?," *National Catholic Reporter*, October 27, 1995.

[16] *Ut Unum Sint*, 34, *Ibid.*, 57.

[17] The intervention actually came from "a letter written by Cardinal Joseph Ratzinger to the bishops' committee charged with drafting a pastoral on women's concerns. The letter was said to have "significantly influenced the outcome of that document." See Thomas J. Smith, "Bishops Urged to Promote More Dialogue: Weakland Joins in Statement to Conference." This article appeared on the "Official" page of the [Milwaukee] *Catholic Herald*, July 13, 1995.

[18] *Ibid.*

[19] *Ut Unum Sint*, 36, 58.

[20] In this sense, I am defining "abuse" in the same way done by the U.S. Bishops in their document, "When I Call for Help: Domestic Violence against Women:" "What is abuse? It is any kind of behavior that one person [I say "anyone" or "any group"] uses to control another through fear and intimidation." See *Origins* 22 (1992), 355.

[21] *Lumen Gentium*, 39, in Flannery, *Ibid.*, 396.

[22] *Ibid*, 48, 408.

[23] "Romanita," in John Deedy, *The Catholic Fact Book* (Chicago: Thomas More, 1986), 377. Deedy concludes that "Romanita is generally used derogatorily." For a further examination on how, in the name of *unity* an ideology is developed by Rome to reinforce its own interpretation of "church," see Dietrich Wiederkehr, "Ortskirche und Weltkirche: fruchtbare Konflikte zwischen bisheriger und weiter furrender Ekklesiopraxie und Ekklesiologie," *Zeitscrift fur Missionswissenschaft und Religionswissenschaft* 68 (1994), 99-115.

[24] Archbishop Geraldo Agnelo, Secretary of the Congregation for Divine Worship, quoted in CNS story in CNT Staff with CNS Files, "Canadian Bishops Defend Inclusive Language Lectionary," *Catholic New Times*, 20 November, 1994, 1.

[25] Richard Sklba, in Ethel M. Gintoft, "Vatican Nixes Translations for Liturgy: Milwaukee Bishop Defends Scholarship of Revised Bible, Psalter Works," *Catholic Herald*, November 10, 1994, 15.

[26] The Curial actions around language were not isolated to the United States. Archbishop Stephen Hamao of Japan, the only Curia official to sign a document in 2002 calling for Pope John Paul II to convene a new ecumenical council, stated: "Everything is still too Roman-centered. . . For example, we in Japan have had very bad experiences with the translation of liturgical texts. We prepared a missal that took 10 years, which then came over to Rome. Since no one [t]here could read Japanese, it was assigned to seminarians who don't have the trust of the bishops' conference." However, they did have the trust of the Curia officials. That is why they would take the text developed by experts and give it to mere seminarians. The issue of trust now is about loyalty to Rome rather than fidelity to the text. See John L. Allen, Jr., "31 Bishops Sign Petition for New Council," *National Catholic Reporter*, May 10, 2002.

[27] Bishop Joseph L. Imesch, quoted in George W. Cornell, "Bishops at Impasse on Role of Women in Church, Society," *The Union-News*, November, 1992.

[28] *Ibid.*

[29] Peter Steinfels, "Catholic Bishops in U.S. Reject Policy Letter on Role of Women: Consensus Eludes Group after 9 Years of Work," *The New York Times*, December 19, 1992, 1.

[30] This was expressed in Pope John Paul II's Apostolic Constitution, *Pastor Bonus,* issued on April 28, 1988 to be effectual March 1, 1989. In the words of a top canonist in the U.S., "On an initial reading, *Pastor Bonus* does not seem to be . . . an especially evident response to the expectations for Curial reform that have been building since the start of the Second Vatican Council. This is regrettable not only because the Petrine ministry deserves better, but because the communion of the Church deserves more." See James H. Provost, *"Pastor Bonus*: Reflections on the Reorganization of the Roman Curia," *The Jurist* 48 (1988), 529.

[31] *Ut Unum Sint,* 16, *Ibid.,* 54.

[32] Ignatius of Antioch.

[33] "Lumen Gentium," 13, in Flannery, *Ibid.,* 364-365. See Sullivan, *Ibid*, 87-88.

[34] Michael H. Crosby, *Celibacy: Means of Control or Mandate of the Heart?* (Notre Dame, IN: Ave Maria, 1996).

[35] See Pamela Schaefer, "Four Jesuits Denied Promotion by Rome," *National Catholic Reporter*, March 29 1996, 5.

[36] Frank Morrisey, OMI, quoted in Terry Dosh, "Canadian Bishops Have Lost Authority!," Bread Rising 13.1 (2003), 3.

[37] Quinn, VIII, *Ibid.,* 124.

[38] "Apodictic," in Jean L. McKechnie, general supervisor, *Webster's New Universal Unabridged Dictionary*, 2nd ed. (Cleveland: Dorset & Baber, 1983), 86.

[39] *Ibid.*, 262, 158.

[40] John Paul II, "Unity of the Church," March 4, 1983, in Alfred T. Hennelly, S.J., *Liberation Theology: A Documentary History* (Maryknoll, NY: Orbis, 1990), 331. See also *The Pope Speaks* 28 (1983), 208.

[41] Most Rev. Donald W. Trautman, "A Biblical Foundation for Collaborative Ministry: Charism, Authority, and Service," Convocation of Priests of the Diocese of Pittsburgh, October 13, 1998.

[42] Pope John Paul II, in *Ut Unum Sint*, refers to this incident in acknowledging the "weakness" of Peter. Number 91, 69.

CHAPTER THREE

The Internal Contradictions Resulting from
Imposed Celibacy

Because of the way Catholic Tradition has evolved and the ideological way the Scriptures have been interpreted to justify mandatory celibacy (especially for diocesan priests and homosexual Catholics [to whom the charism of celibacy has been "given"]), we now face a host of "internal contradictions" in the present approach to celibacy. Because celibacy has been used to establish and maintain patriarchy within the Catholic Church, I do not believe the issues will be seriously addressed by those in power, since it has served their interests that we remain in the present situation. Consequently, this chapter will address these internal contradictions. Assuming material in chapter one, I will highlight the consequences of continuing them. While I will emphasize their expressions among diocesan priests, deacons and homosexual Catholics, I will begin by noting contradictions involving celibacy for "consecrated" members of religious congregations like me. My remarks refer especially to men in these three groups in places like Western Europe and North America, Australia and New Zealand.[1]

Implications for Members of Religious Congregations

In 1959 when I joined the Capuchin Franciscans, I never thought of entering the separate novitiate the province operated for lay brothers. I just assumed I would become a priest in the Order. So, when I visited the Capuchin contact person asking for entrance into the novitiate, the only clarifying question he asked me was not: "Why don't you want to be a lay brother," but "Why don't you want to be a diocesan priest?" My response was straight and simple: "Because religious priests go all the way." He did not challenge my rationale.

In the church that had nurtured me priesthood was the highest "calling," the closest one could get to Christ. Religious priesthood took that call a step higher, to the highest state of perfection–unless, of course, you were "called" to be a bishop!

My way of thinking was colored by another dynamic related to church discipline and practice at that time: the virtual limitation of any and all ministries and positions of leadership in the church to those men who would embrace the diocesan priesthood or religious life. Thus, the *most effective* way one could respond to the baptismal mission was to become a priest or religious. Any other "calling" seemed second-best, if a vocation at all.

In addition to flawed theological and pastoral reasons supporting religious priesthood, there were less noble motives as well. It was prestigious in that generation to "choose" to enter the priesthood or religious life. The wider Catholic community honored its members who did so, especially if the community was ethnic. Often joining the seminary or "the monastery" also represented a way of upward mobility. These Catholic entities offered better educational opportunities than those in the secular world, especially for men or women from poorer families or families with several children. Such unconscious motivation, I believe, may help one understand why so many may be entering religious congregations (as well as diocesan seminaries) in developing nations today.

In the late 1950s when I entered the seminary, almost every congregation found itself building a novitiate or some kind of formation house. Dioceses started massive development drives for the expansion of their seminaries. However, within a little more than one generation, the novitiates have become retreat centers, monastery wings have become retirement houses and expanded seminaries have become chancery offices. Concurrently, the daily prayers in the liturgy for "vocations to the priesthood and religious life" are multiplied, vocation recruiters burn out and the remaining members watch helplessly as the median age increases. Meanwhile, many of the "young ones" come to the more traditional congregations and dioceses seeking stability and greater meaning, stay for a few years and leave, often for the same reasons the original group left: celibacy. Many young priests remaining seem more concerned about their "ontological" (essential) uniqueness that separates them from God's people than what makes them part of them.[2]

With less priests many bishops scour the Philippines and Poland, Africa and Asia recruiting priests. Sadly, some coming sexually relate to women in the same ways some others in their native countries still do; others abuse the power of their office. In some diocese the results have become quite sordid.

The lack of "vocations" today leads some to a type of "blame the victim" mentality; others question what may be wrong with them and/or their group. Rather than consider what may have been mitigating motives defining past expressions of celibacy and spurred by the memory of huge numbers, some hearken back to notions of the "good old days." Those of us in religious orders deny the need to interpret in a new way the signs of the times that might recapture evangelically the prophetic dimension of religious life in a way that challenges both society and church when either's ways become abusive. So we inaugurate new vocation programs based on a former way of life that probably will never rise again (except in those newly-founded groups that stress more rigid ways). We forget that when Jesus' understanding of celibacy becomes the norm (in its expanded meaning), there will not be many celibates. Did he not imply that it was only natural that few would accept celibacy? Why do we still insist that our way of life based on celibacy can be the exception to his understanding?

Many of the same dynamics can be found in diocesan personnel concerned about "vocations." Despite good numbers, in some places, of seminarians, U.S. data shows that the "desire to marry is one of the main factors leading seminarians to quit studying for the priesthood."[3] In fact, the most-stated reasons for leaving offered by (former) seminarians referred to negative attitudes toward celibacy and a desire to marry.

Contradictions about the "Evangelical Counsels"

In the past those "evangelical counsels" defined as poverty, chastity and obedience were seen as the common thread linking the disparate forms of the consecrated life. The very word "evangelical" points to the *fact* that they should find their basis in the life of Jesus as detailed in the gospels. Yet, as we recall chapter one's rejection of Matthew 19 as a basis for celibacy (in the strict sense as it refers to the vowed life) and, as one probes the gospels further, it can be questioned whether the present forms of obedience and poverty prescribed for those in the "consecrated life" truly have parallels in the life or teachings of the Gospel Jesus. Increasingly I wonder whether any of the "evangelical counsels" can be found clearly in the *evangelion.*

First, our obedience as religious differs vastly from that of Jesus. His obedience as an adult was not to any human being (as is ours), but to God. He did not obey God via another acting in God's name. Our form of religious obedience in our promises or vows has arisen historically within the institutional church. It is made to leaders in the particular institute who get their authority from Rome or the local bishop. Ultimately, the obedience goes up the ladder to the pope, seen as the successor to Peter. I don't recall Jesus obeying Peter anywhere. So, if our obedience is "evangelical" because it is grounded in Jesus' example of submission, and since he submitted to no human being or religious leader, we will look long before we find examples of "evangelical" obedience in the gospels.

The traditional scriptural warrants defining poverty as an evangelical counsel also raise serious questions. The continually proffered scriptural passages like Matthew 8:20 and 19:21 which have been used to justify a vow of poverty actually have more to do with basic requirements for anyone considering discipleship. At least in Matthew, the discipleship that demands a re-ordering of one's life toward the poor is not a counsel; it is an essential requirement for all who would follow Jesus as baptized Christians. Discipleship demands solidarity with the poor as an inseparable dimension. All discipleship, not religious life only, demands reordering one's life on behalf of the poor.

Furthermore, in the texts from the Hebrew Scriptures which the scriptures identify with Jesus, especially those from Isaiah, the "evangelical counsel" which seems more important than poverty is justice. In fact, as the parable of the Last Judgment points out, being "just" toward the poor will be the sign of our sharing in the reign of God (Mt 25:3146). Perhaps, in light of the injustice so rampant in our world--including poverty--justice is more at the heart of being an evangelical person today than poverty. But few religious today are involved in social justice work, and those who are often find conflicts with church authorities when they link issues of justice with aberrations in the institutional church. Furthermore, with the clerical group in control of all charisms, any prophetic witness by any religious must be open to that group's *fiat*.

Consequently, as I read the scriptures, the only real counsel of the traditional "three evangelical counsels" seems to be that related to the option for celibacy. Furthermore, its evangelical base, as noted in chapter one, can only be promoted if the Matthew 19 text will be interpreted in its wider sense. Given this understanding, such freely-embraced celibacy must constitute the heart of any and all forms of consecrated life. Thus Edward Schillebeeckx stated: "Strictly speaking, there is only one evangelical counsel in the gospel ... therefore Christian celibacy is the only evangelical counsel properly so called and is left entirely up to the will of the individual Christian."[4]

Some may disagree with the contradictions I have raised about the "consecrated life" and celibacy. I'd like to be around a century from now to see whether they will prove to be faulty or true. However, I am sure that, if celibacy must always be seen as the sine-qua-non of consecrated life, it also must be de-linked from its mandatory identification with the diocesan priesthood if the church will be faithful to Jesus' evangelical teaching.

Implications for the Diocesan Priesthood

Of the world's 218,000 parishes, 105,000 have no resident priest. In the U.S.A. the number of priests has dropped from 58,632 in 1965 to 44,874 in 2002. At the same time the number of Catholics has increased from 45.6 million to 62.6 million. In Canada there was a 23 percent loss in the number of priests from 1990 – 2003; the Catholic population increased by 10 percent. Meanwhile diocese after diocese has to close parishes or build larger parishes that are being consolidated.

In a cover issue addressing issues related to the second round of clergy abuse, *Time* magazine presented (April 1, 2002) "Troubling Trends" associated with the increasing number of people in the pews and the decreasing number of priests to serve them. Statistically grounded, the data showed that:

In the U.S., with the growth in the number of Catholics, especially Latinos.

– the ranks of priests and nuns are thinning;

– and they're getting older. More priests are over 90 than under 30. 27% of parishes have no resident priest;

– and while the number studying to become priests has fallen;

– the church as been using more deacons to take up the slack..[5]

That the future does not auger well regarding an increase in priests was evident around the same time when the Center for Applied Research in the Apostolate (CARA) issued its annual "Catholic Ministry Formation Enrollments: Statistical Overview for 2001-2002." Priestly formation enrollments for 2001-2002 were "at approximately the same level as they were a decade ago," although they were 3% higher than the year before.[6]

A 1972 University of Notre Dame dissertation discussed *The Differences between Priests Legally and Personally Committed to Celibacy.* Personal celibates were those having a balance between their inner psychic spiritual life and the law of the institutional church. Of the 1,256 priests surveyed, a marked difference appeared between priests living celibacy because of the law and those who did so freely. These viewed themselves as part of the "participation mystique within the organizational church."[7] A legal celibate was defined as "a mere conformist or as one who is being expelled from the participation mystique and beginning to question the meaning of celibacy."[8] The data showed that priests identified as legal celibates had a higher score on anomie than priests identified as personal celibates:

> 1. Priests identified as legal celibates had a lower score on belief in celibacy than priests identified as personal celibates.
> 2. Priests identified as legal celibates had a lower score on attitudes towards celibacy than priests identified as personal celibates.
> 3. Priests identified as legal celibates had a lower score on the personal cost of changing the celibate commitment than priests identified as personal celibates.
> 4. Priests identified as legal celibates had a higher score on "dating behavior" than those identified as personal celibates.[9]

The priest-author of the dissertation concluded that, because celibacy is a gift from God, it "cannot be legislated for an entire group without risking the exposure of a good number of individuals to serious psychological problems." Noting that celibacy offers value for individuals only when it is freely chosen and freely lived, he concluded: "Psychological growth is the result of choice, and choice requires a clear, conscious evaluation of the options."[10]

In a twenty-five-year clergy study, A. W. Richard Sipe discovered that, of those priests he counseled or interviewed for his research, only ten percent admitted to no problems with celibacy. He learned that half of the American priests suffer from psychological immaturity or sexual difficulties.[11] While Sipe's methods as well as his conclusions have been challenged by some, they are confirmed when church leaders privately speak from their hearts. This must be kept in mind when we read about the many young priests today who profess greater happiness in the priesthood than their predecessors.[12]

Most of the 80,000 priests who left the active ministry between 1965 and 2000 have been granted dispensations by the Vatican. A main reason priests and religious men proffer as they seek dispensations revolves around "psychological immaturity;" this prevented them from making a free choice. This rationale must have merit in the eyes of church leaders in the Vatican in order for men to be granted dispensations in those numbers.

Despite Pope John Paul II's belief that celibacy has grounds in the call to discipleship and that the "ideal was affirmed" with increasing consistency during church history, he seems to find nothing contradictory in accepting converted married clergymen (primarily Anglican and Lutheran) as Latin Rite priests and having them remain married. Under his papacy more married priests from such denominations have been accepted into the Latin Rite than in any other period since the twelfth century. Further, the fact that they need not be celibate in their marriages indicates the Vatican acknowledges there is nothing inherent in the priesthood that demands celibacy.

In the first chapter I showed that the former cultic reasons once justifying priestly celibacy no longer hold. Thus any laws based on such faulty rationales will be weak indeed. In the words of I. Morsdorff, "In order for a law to have obligatory force, it must be a reasonable ordinance. With regard to whether it can be followed, a law is reasonable when what it commands is not merely physically but morally possible, and that possibility must be determined with regard to the capacity of the person affected. *Ad impossible nemo tenetur.*"[13] Building on Morsdorff's insights, Heinz-Jurgen Vogels concludes:

> Since the charism, the "capacity" for a celibate life, is not at the disposal of the individual affected, the law exceeds the capacity of many persons subject to it. For all those who do not have the charism, no legal obligation comes into force. Since, however, the law is intended to be binding on all priests, but not all priests have the charism. . . the law cannot reach its objective of obliging all priests to be celibate. It must, therefore, be repealed as an "unreasonable, irrational law."[14]

I define violence as any force that inflicts injury. Where force controls, there can be no full or authentic freedom. Where there is coercion, there is control. Where one must submit to another without real freedom, autonomy is jeopardized. Liberty gets compromised whenever constraint undermines choice. All of these contradictions result when people are compelled by a compulsory law. If this is so, compulsory celibacy for priests represents a canonized form of institutional violence. This canonized violence is manifest in the way Canon Law makes a cleric's sex with a grown woman more serious than sex with a minor. The priest-canonist Thomas Doyle comments: "Even occasional acts of sex with a minor are far more devastating than habitual sexual contact with a consenting adult of either gender." He goes on to show the deeper, institutionalized form of violence in the law when he says that it shows "more concern for the clerical establishment than for the victim."[15]

Meanwhile more and more Catholic parishes suffer, unable to celebrate their identities as eucharistic communities. Any effort to change runs into stone walls of resistance. This seems clear from an experience with the Vatican in my own archdiocese of Milwaukee.

In 1991 our then-Archbishop, Rembert Weakland, wrote a pastoral letter on the future of parishes in Milwaukee.

In the draft he wrote: "It seems inevitable that we will in a few years, if not sooner, reach a point when the number of priests will not be able to handle the 285 parishes and missions of the archdiocese (in 2002 down to 226 parishes). We cannot be assured that all parishes will have full eucharistic celebrations or Mass every Sunday." Seeing "no other way out of this very difficult situation," he offered an alternative--the ordination of married men--if certain conditions would be fulfilled:

> if a parish that cannot have a regular Mass on Sundays because of the shortage of priests remains faithful in assembling each Sunday for the Liturgy of the Word, presided over by a lay minister or a deacon, and with the distribution of holy communion outside of Mass only on rare occasions such as feasts, lest it become habitual and be seen as a normal substitute for the Mass;
>
> and if the parish continues to have all the characteristics described in the first section of this document,

namely, worship and a sacramental perspective that is a part of their theology and practice whenever possible, education at all levels, and outreach to the needy;

and if the parish has an active vocation program for the celibate priesthood;

and if it seems this state of affairs may continue for many years, perhaps into the next decade, then I would be willing to help the community surface a qualified candidate for ordained priesthood--even if a married man--and, without raising false expectations or unfounded hopes for him or the community, present such a candidate to the Pastor of the Universal Church for light and guidance. In such a case we would have done all possible at the local level and could feel that we had been responsible stewards of God's goods and graces. If the strength of the Church then should diminish here because of the continued lack of ordained priests and sacramental opportunities for the faithful, our consciences could remain in peace. We had done our best.[16]

Archbishop Weakland also sent this "draft" to the Vatican. In the final form of the letter published the following November, the archbishop wrote: "I was informed by the Vatican Secretariat of State that my suggestion of proposing a married man was regarded as 'out of place.'" The Secretariat noted that: "As a result of the recent Synod, an appropriate Apostolic Exhortation is under preparation in which the Supreme Pontiff will offer the universal church orientations and directives to face adequately the same delicate issue. We look forward to the publication of that document."[17]

More than ten years later, with more parishes closing or merging, no directions have been given "to face adequately the . . . delicate issue." Again preserving the male, celibate model of the clergy seems more important than the needs of the local church.

Without even addressing the greater lack of priests in developing nations, the Vatican's nonaction on the subject of the same "delicate issue" of "eucharist-less" parishes has not been "adequate" for the needs of Canadian people either. Some years after the Vatican promise, a group of Canadian bishops went to Rome for their *ad limina* visit. Men serving as missionaries in their sparsely populated areas were dying or leaving without replacements. Fewer diocesan priests were available for these and other remote areas. So they brought their case directly to Pope John Paul II. "We explained our plight to him. And we gave all our reasons why the people have a greater right to the eucharist than we have in limiting the priesthood to celibates," Bishop Remi De Roo explained to me. He said that the Pope pounded the desk, "all along saying: 'Deus *providebit'* (God will provide)." "But," Bishop De Roo, countered: "God has not provided and God will not provide. Somehow the Pope seems to think that by saying *Deus providebit,* the problem will go away. Well, it hasn't gone away and we are left with the eucharist-less communities. Whose problem is it? God's or the Pope's?"

In his conversation with me, Bishop De Roo pointed to a deeper issue going beyond the Pope's way of addressing the crisis of celibacy; the structural issue arising from a consequence of being unable to challenge such a mindset because of the notion of infallibility that has come to cloak almost everything uttered by a pope. The Canadian bishop indicated how, what he perceived as blindness in the Vatican on the issue of married priests, raises a serious question. How can people believe that they possess all truth? A consequence of this attitude, he noted, gets expressed in the worst forms of fundamentalism. "When people believe they alone possess the whole truth and that God gives them that power, are they not in effect inclined to play God? So 'God' has to support what they say or make right their wrongs. It's all so contradictory," the bishop said. Is not such thinking, he said, the kind of thinking that ultimately leads to fanaticism? Fanatics totally believe what they alone say is true. Their truth is true. But it may be true only from their limited, culturally-conditioned viewpoint. The greater truth requires the discernment of the entire community of believers.

In his 2002 World Day of Peace statement, Pope John Paul II himself seemed to echo the thoughts of Remi de Roo. He wrote that

> fanatic *fundamentalism* . . . springs from the conviction that one's own vision of the truth must be forced upon everyone else. Instead, even when the truth has been reached—and this

can happen only in a limited and imperfect way—it can never be imposed. Respect for a persons's conscience, where the image of God himself is reflected (cf. *Gen* 1:26-27), means that we can only propose the truth to others, who are then responsible for accepting it.[18]

At the meeting above noted by Bishop de Roo, another Canadian bishop, Denis Croteau of the Mackenzie-Fort Smith diocese told the Pope that in some ethnic communities (e.g., among the Inuit and Dene peoples of northern Canada) an unmarried priest is unable to be a leader (as is the case in many African nations): "The idea is that these people have a family value in their culture that, unless you are married, you're not a leader and people won't listen to you." He said: "If you have married and raised a family, then you're an elder, a man of experience. Then you can talk and people will respect your position."[19] His argument carried no weight.

Rather than make an exception for married priests in such a culture, it seems the Vatican is willing to refuse to adapt to the cultural norms of certain native peoples in order to preserve the clerical norm of patriarchal celibacy. Cardinal Jozef Tomko, head of the Congregation for the Evangelization of Peoples, reportedly said that any exception granted in Canada "could not remain an exception" and would open a floodgate of similar requests in Africa, South America and elsewhere.[20] So the rule stands, even if it be at the expense of many cultures.

Implications for Married Deacons

A related example of internal contradictions and confusing messages from the Vatican related to celibacy can be found in the demand that permanent deacons promise not to re-marry should their spouses die.

Once I met a young-looking permanent deacon. Though very involved in parish ministry, at the same time he was quite outspoken regarding many things happening in the institutional church, especially related to women's issues. Despite his position on such matters, he did not seem to see how some of the unfair rulings of the institutional church might apply to himself and his own situation. When I pointed out that the rule requiring him to promise celibacy if his wife died made him a victim of a purely disciplinary ruling, he looked surprised. He said he never really thought about it.

"Why did you promise not to remarry if anything happened to Helen?" I asked.

"Well, I guess I just love her so much I couldn't imagine myself ever marrying anyone else. So it was easy to make the promise," he responded. Then he got quite pensive. He added: "I guess I just bought the package too. I so much wanted to help people as a deacon that I never really thought about the consequences for me and my own future as a man."

A week later I had dinner with two other permanent deacons and one of their wives. I asked them why they accepted not being able to remarry when they committed themselves to be deacons. One of them said: "I am so involved with my wife that, at this point, I just can't imagine having anyone else but her in my life. So making that promise, given my situation, was very easy." It was almost an echo of the younger deacon. The other one said: "I believe my promise was just part of the package. You have to relativize it."

The more I listened, the more I discovered a great disconnect: when ordained, the deacon who is married receives the fullness of grace to be faithful to that ministry in the church, precisely as a married man (who is assumed to be having genital relations with his wife). However, should his wife die, it is presumed that the man gets another grace from God to be celibate. Thus celibacy is not the "gift" given at ordination to married men who become deacons; it somehow appears at the deaths of their wives. Such seems to be the logic that guides such arbitrary and unnecessary disciplines.

Implications for Homosexual Catholics

After many communications related to homosexuality from various U.S. bishops,[21] in 1986 the Congregation for the Doctrine of the Faith (CDF) issued a letter to the bishops of the Catholic Church on "The Pastoral Care of Homosexual Persons." The letter's title indicates the Vatican willingness to admit that homosexuality represents the reality of some persons in the church. This document was reinforced with another statement in 1992. An earlier "Declaration on Certain Questions Concerning Sexual Ethics" (1975) recognized that homosexual persons were "definitively such because of some kind of innate instinct or a pathological constitution judged to be incurable."[22]

The 1986 letter achieved something of a "first" in a Vatican statement. It stated that the homosexual reality in people may be a "given," not something they have chosen (even though a 1976 letter of the U.S. bishops already accepted the "through no fault of their own" argument).[23]

The 1986 and 1992 statements said that the homosexual orientation "must be seen as an objective disorder,"[24] and that the homosexual reality represents "a more or less strong tendency ordered toward an intrinsic moral evil." Since one's sexuality grounds one's personality, these statements strongly imply that homosexual persons are constitutively disordered. Furthermore, the documents indicated that, when one is oriented by nature to be sexually attracted toward someone of the same sex, that person is objectively ordered toward intrinsic evil.

The consequence of these teachings for homosexual people sincere about their discipleship was articulated by William Shannon with devastating honesty:

> Whether one agrees with this position or does not, it is not difficult to see the psychological damage that could be done to a person by telling him or her that his or her very person was ordered toward intrinsic moral evil. It would be like telling someone that he or she is carrying a moral time bomb. It would be to say that such a person is a constant proximate occasion of sin to himself or herself.[25]

In the same context of stating that the homosexual orientation is an "objective disorder," the CDF statement makes it clear that homosexual persons have an "intrinsic dignity" that "must always be respected in word, in action, and in law."[26] Commenting on this part of the letter in light of its overall thrust, the National Board of the

Conference of Major Superiors of Men declared: "This . . . is neither helpful nor enlightening."[27] I would add it also is confusing, condescending and contradictory.

How can anyone having an "objective" disorder also have an "intrinsic" dignity? What distinguishes that which is "objective" and "intrinsic?" Don't both words refer to the constitutive dimension of one's very person which is made in the divine image? Doesn't anyone or anything objectively disordered lack some kind of intrinsic dignity? Furthermore the documents imply that when one's sexuality (and therefore, personality) is constitutionally oriented toward persons of the same sex, that person is objectively ordered toward an intrinsic evil. Also, if one accepts the divine activity in the creation of every person, then has God created homosexual persons with an objective disorder? Admitting the all-pervasiveness of original sin, why are homosexual persons alone created with such a sinful orientation? Are only heterosexual persons God's images with no objective disorder?

What do the CDF conclusions say about God's "choice" process? If God has chosen this group to be created with an objective disorder and with an orientation naturally ordered toward moral evil, could not God be accused of doing them harm or, at least, being an accomplice in their sin when they relate to others genitally? How can God choose to create homosexual persons with "a more or less strong tendency ordered toward an intrinsic moral evil" in such a way that "the inclination itself must be seen as an objective disorder?"[28] More than saying anything about a "disordered" creature, it would indict the disordered ways of the Creator!

The Reluctance to Healthily Address the Reality of Homosexual Men in Church Ministry

At this point it seems appropriate that another issue filled with contradictions related to celibacy—homosexuals and/or gays in the clergy--be addressed. This very sensitive and complex issue has been repressed and resisted, denied and demeaned at the institutional level for too long. It involves the disproportionate number of homosexuals in seminaries, among the newly ordained and veteran priests, as well as the apparently even larger numbers entering and belonging to institutes of the consecrated life.

More than a decade ago, in *The Dysfunctional Church: Addiction and Codependency in the Family of Catholicism,* I tried to address this phenomenon prudently and honestly. Given the paucity, then as well as now, of accurate accounting (because of episcopal resistance to garner the true facts), I said:

> North American data suggests that among the clergy at least thirty percent are homosexual in their orientation. On the other hand, these increasing numbers of men must remain closeted and repressed--denying who they are--because of the climate of homophobia that comes from the Vatican. When the various unhealthy symptoms in a closed, dysfunctional family dominate (no-talk rule, internalized feelings, unspoken expectations, entangled relationships), it is no wonder bishops and major superiors seem paralyzed by this phenomenon of ever-increasing numbers of homosexuals seeking admission to seminaries, priesthood, and religious life.[29]

I stated that, since the Second Vatican Council, despite the secretly acknowledged higher numbers of homosexuals in the priesthood and male religious congregations, bishops and major superiors have not found healthy ways to help them in their lives and ministry. To me, the increasing numbers of homosexuals entering the priesthood and religious life is not a "problem," as some would insist. In my mind any "problem" connected with this issue can be linked to the ways denial and dissociation work in the institutional church and culture that keep the reality from being addressed clearly, cleanly and creatively.

A reason some homosexuals go to seminaries and enter formation programs arises from the fact that, because they have heard enough gay-bashing from the leaders of the institutional church, they co-dependently are attracted to the very forces that will abuse them more. Others enter with repressed homosexual feelings; without realizing it they are attracted to an all-male group. Still others feel they will be supported to live in a way that will keep them from facing that which they reject in themselves. Other men, more honest insofar as they declare themselves gay (and thus become more healthy for being public about it in some way), hope they might be encouraged in life-giving ways to deepen their celibacy. Whatever the reasons may be, once they enter, because the leaders fail to address the reality and offer healthy ways to help men live celibately in an all-male fraternity, there can be a tendency to be influenced by other factors, including some negative elements in the gay subculture.

A tendency of oppressed groups to find meaning and support among their own members can be found in subcultures that exist in wider cultures of repression. While this can be very healthy and necessary, it also can contain a shadow-side in the form of exclusionary dynamics which undermine community. In such gatherings, boundary lines get drawn. When such dynamics take place, people out of the "in group" may either become homophobic or find their homophobia "validated." Even when the sub-groups are not exclusive, they can be perceived as a threat because of homophobia and/or projection by others who have not addressed their own latent homosexuality.

Another consequence of having increasing numbers of repressed homosexuals rather than healthy gays in the priesthood and religious life has only begun to surface as our Catholic clergy moves from being defined as heterosexual to being increasingly homosexual. Social psychologists, aware of what happens when oppressed peoples use power when it is given to them, recently have pointed to a phenomenon already occurring in some religious groups: the arbitrary way some homosexuals or gays entering positions of leadership can exercise authority.

A gay priest friend of mine recently told me about his own experience of mistreatment at the hands of some of the very men in the chancery who were closeted gays. He said: "Because they've been hurt by the old rules (about homosexuals in the church) that were stacked against them, and because they've been repressed for so long, these new leaders don't play by the old rules. There's nothing consistent. You are either in their favor or out of it. It all depends on whether they like you or not."

In too many instances, I find the institutional response to such data is one of denial, delusion and dissociation. Once, after meeting with the North American provincials of an international group of religious men, the host-provincial expressed shock at learning that, in my province at that time, some of the gay friars had organized themselves into a support group. In those years (the early 80s) it was quite unique for any group of religious men to have anything like a "gay caucus." In response to his shock, I said: "All of us have gays and good numbers of them. At least our province admits it and tries to respond to it in a healthy way."

"We would never do anything like that in our congregation," he responded.

"Why not?," I asked.

"Because we don't have that problem," he insisted.

For some time, this man's province had gone without any men joining it. However, just a few months before, three novices had made first profession. One of them had come to the gathering of the provincials that I had attended at which the provincial and I had the discussion. On the way back to his place of residence in another state, he was apprehended by the police. A young man, a minor, had reported that he had solicited him for sex. Just three months out of the novitiate, the newly professed celibate was sent immediately for treatment. Ultimately he left, or was forced to leave.

A half year later the other two announced they were going to leave the Order–together. They had fallen in love with each other and wanted to cohabit. Their departure would leave the province with no men in temporary vows. So much for not having any "problem" in his province! That provincial has now become a bishop.

One of the greatest obstacles to honestly addressing the issue of homosexuality by ecclesiastical leaders involves the fact that many of them, provincials and bishops, may be homosexual themselves. While some may have admitted their orientation to a few close friends, they fear "coming out" lest they be rejected by their peers or the public. Still others live with repressed homosexual feelings. Whatever the case, all live in some kind of fear and intimidation that they might be "outed" or told to "get out." Others fear that, if they address the issue in a healthy and constructive way, they may be challenged about their own orientation, questioned about possible past behavior or marginated. So silence shrouded in secrecy sustains the shame of being considered "different." Despite all the forms of denial, the need to address the situation of increasing numbers of homosexuals in the clergy and religious life, as well as the need to do so creatively and humanely grows stronger.

The resistance to making changes in the celibacy law that keeps many heterosexuals from entering priestly ministry will not diminish the situation either. I have met too many straight men who resist the priesthood and religious life because they don't want to get caught up in an environment they perceive to be concerned more about issues having to do with the gay life than the spiritual life.

Another situation that begs for honest discussion involves the reductionistic way that many simplistically and wrongly equate the pedophilia and ephebophilia problems in the Catholic Church with the fact that there are a high percentage of gays among the clergy and in religious congregations of men.

During the first round of allegations of pedophilia among the clergy, a Chicago study in the early 1990s concluded that about 40 of 2,200 priests, less than 2 percent, committed sexual misconduct with a minor. Only one victim was prepubescent.[30] Thus, in the first round of pedophilia, almost all priests accused of legal pedophilia vis-a-vis minors were, psychologically-speaking, ephebophiles (ie, oriented to same-sex pubescents). Furthermore, other data shows no higher incidence of legal pedophilia among homosexuals than others. Given this fact, the parallel fact that there *is* a higher numbers of gays in the priesthood cannot be simply dismissed as "homophobia" when we consider why so many priests (among the so few of the perpetrators) abused adolescent boys rather than prepubescents.

Why? Some may point to parallels to the "Lolita Syndrome" that may exist among homosexual or gay priests insofar as they are oriented toward adolescent boys rather than adolescent girls, as are their straight counterparts. Others say some priests were perpetrators because of arrested sexual development. Yet professionals point elsewhere. Reasons can be found in the fact that, since most priests who abuse children have been abused themselves, it is a kind of re-enactment of their own abuse and may have little connection to their sexual orientation.[31] Others point to the homosocial (in contrast to the homosexual) culture of the priesthood itself. Then some note the unconscious attempt to escape their own sexuality. Still others find a rationale around convenience (ie, until only recently only boys were altar servers) and the priests' role as male mentors. Others note that the laity has traditionally deferred to priests. A few even suggest the abuse of boys might arise from a fear of women.

Some conservatives have tried to make a causal link between the higher number of gays in the priesthood and religious life and the fact that the victims of clergy abuse were primarily adolescent boys, not younger children.[32] But linking pedophilia with homosexuals in the priesthood has no founding in fact and cannot be made into a scapegoat solution.[33] While they may be right in saying, with William Donohue, President of the Catholic League for Religious and Civil Rights, that the church's hierarchy have been derelict in their duty,[34] their concern about rising numbers of gays in the ministry is bogus, especially when they try to link being gay with being an abuser.

A professional insight from the Dominican psychologist, Joseph Guido, seems closer to an answer. He notes:

> Although reliable statistics are hard to come by, anecdotal reports suggest that there are a higher percentage of homosexually oriented individuals in the priesthood than in society generally. If so, then it is reasonable to expect that among those priests who abuse adolescents a higher proportion will be gay, not because gay individuals as such are predisposed to offend, but because there are more gay men in the priesthood. The inclination to abuse a minor proceeds from multiple factors and is only incidentally related to sexual orientation. It would be wrong to exclude a man from holy orders on the basis of sexual orientation alone in an attempt to stem the abuse of children and adolescents.[35]

Theological Contradictions Regarding the "Call" to Celibacy

How can one adequately address theologically such contradictions around imposed celibacy for priests and gays? The *Catechism of the Catholic Church* includes "chastity" among the fruits of the Holy Spirit.[36] Yet, the *Catechism's* approach to chastity is not clear. On the one hand, it seems to mean the same as celibacy insofar as both are treated from the perspective of having no genital sex. On the other, three groups--those in consecrated life, diocesan priests and homosexual persons--are "called" in one way or another to celibacy.

To expand on this contradiction, consider the following argument: First, the *Catechism* makes it clear the consecrated life involves a call. It states:

> The perfection of charity, to which all the faithful are called, entails for those who freely follow the call to consecrated life the obligation of practicing chastity in celibacy for the sake of the Kingdom, poverty and obedience. It is the profession of these counsels, within a permanent state of life recognized by the Church, that characterizes the life consecrated to God."[37]

The *Catechism* also says that priests, those in our second group, are "called" to celibacy as well:

> All the ordained ministers of the Latin Church, with the exception of permanent deacons, are normally chosen from among men of faith who live a celibate life and who intend to remain celibate "for the sake of the kingdom of heaven" (Mt 19:12). Called to consecrate themselves with undivided heart to the Lord and to "the affairs of the Lord" (1 Cor 7:32), they give themselves entirely to God and to men.[38]

It might be expected that the notion of "call" would solely be identified with the celibacy of religious and even secular priests, given the current institutional theology. However, and surprisingly for the first time (to my knowledge) and in an official document of the magnitude of the *Catechism,* homosexual persons also seem to have received the call. "Homosexual persons are called to chastity," the text declares.[39] This leads me to ask: Is this chastity the same as celibacy in the eyes of the teaching church? If so, does this mean homosexual people have been "raised" to the level of priests and religious? Is this some kind of new status the institutional church has ascribed to those who are homosexual? Is the call to be celibate the *same* for religious, for priests and for homosexuals? Why do celibacy and chastity get identified with a vow for one, with a gift-request for another and a constitutive imperative for a third? Why is it that it is a gift to be prayed for by priests and a call imposed on homosexuals and gays?

The contradictions discussed in this chapter regarding the effort of the institutional church to impose celibacy point to a deeper issue: the contradictions around sexuality itself. The crisis in the Roman Church that began with *Humanae Vitae*, the birth control encyclical, which reached a critical point in the two rounds of pedophilia and which now has some in the Vatican calling for a refusal of admission or dismissal of all homosexuals in priesthood and religious life must be faced if the leaders are to regain their credibility. Richard McBrien has stated trenchantly that "celibacy is only one element in a larger network of church regulations and teachings regarding human sexuality and marriage. Many, in fact, view the church's approach as simply one of prohibition."[40] Another approach must be charted.

To concentrate on the prohibition approach would take us in another direction than I have chosen here. What begs to be examined, in light of the above, is the conflicting ways so many in the clergy and male religious congregations have expressed their celibacy in unhealthy ways. It is to this task that we move to in the next two chapters.

Chapter Notes

[1] I am limiting my remarks about celibacy to religious, priests, and homosexual people and do not include single people or widow(er)s for the simple reason that, unfortunately, I have not had much experience with this group. While I may have theoretical notions to

share, I am void of many concrete exemplifications. My approach to writing comes from a praxis that integrates experience and theory. This, unfortunately, has not been available for me as regards single and widowed people in the church. However, I do believe the notions herein are apropos to these groupings.

[2] Dean R. Hoge and Jacqueline E. Wenger, "Changing Commitments and Attitudes of Catholic Priests, 1970-2001," in Jerry Filteau, "Study Says Today's Younger Priests Are Like Older Priests of '70s," [Milwaukee] *Catholic Herald*, March 21, 2002.

[3] "Desire to Marry Seen as Key Factor in Priest Shortage, Survey Reveals," CNS item in [Milwaukee] *Catholic Herald*, April 4, 1990.

[4] Edward Schillebeeckx, *Celibacy*, tr. C. A. L. Jarrott (New York: Sheed and Ward, 1968), 89.

[5] "Troubling Trends," *Time*, April 1, 2002, 33.

[6] Mary L. Gautier, Ph.D., ed., *Catholic Ministry Formation Enrollments: Statistical Overview for 2001-2002* (Washington, D.C.: Center for Applied Research in the Apostolate, 2002), 1.

[7] Rev. Robert J. Loftus, B.A., M.A., *The Differences between Priests Legally and Personally Committed to Celibacy* (Notre Dame, IN: Department of Graduate Studies in Education, 1992), 62.

[8] *Ibid.*

[9] *Ibid.*, ii-iii.

[10] *Ibid.*, iii.

[11] A. W. Richard Sipe, A Secret World: Sexuality and the Search for Celibacy (New York: Brunner/Mazel,1990). See also, A. W. Richard Sipe, Sex, Priests, and Power: Anatomy of a Crisis (New York: Brunner/Mazel, 1995).

[12] Dean R. Hoge and Jacqueline E. Wenger, "Changing Commitments and Attitudes of Catholic Priests, 1970-2001," in Jerry Filteau, "Study Says Today's Younger Priests Are Like Older Priests of '70s," [Milwaukee] *Catholic Herald*, March 21, 2002.

[13] I. Morsdorff, in Heinz-J. Vogels Celibacy–Gift or Law? A Critical Investigation (Kansas City, MO: Sheed & Ward, 1993), 84.

[14] Vogels, *Ibid.,* 66.

[15] Thomas Doyle, quoted in Richard N. Ostling, "Sex Rules for Priests Harsh on Adultery," Associated Press Story, April 19, 2002.

[16] Most Reverend Rembert G. Weakland, O.S.B., "Facing the Future with Hope," First Draft, nos. 39 and 50, [Milwaukee] *Catholic Herald*, January 7, 1991.

[17] Archbishop Rembert G. Weakland, O.S.B., "Facing the Future with Hope: A Pastoral Letter on Parishes for the People of the Archdiocese of Milwaukee," 10, November 1, 1991 (Milwaukee: Archdiocese of Milwaukee, 1991), 4.

[18] Pope John Paul II, Message for the Celebration of the World Day of Peace, 1 January, 2002, 6. http://www.vatican.va/holy_father/john_paul_ii_messages/peace/documents/hf_jp-ii_mes_2.

[19] Bishop Denis Croteau, quoted in "Canadian Bishops Want Married Native Priests," *The Toronto Catholic Register*, October 2, 1993.

[20] Cardinal Jozef Tomko, quoted in Croteau, *Ibid.*

[21] See John Gallagher, ed., *Homosexuality and the Magisterium: Documents from the Vatican and the U.S. Bishops 1975-1985* (Mt. Rainier, MD: New Ways Ministry, 1986).

[22] The Sacred Congregation for the Doctrine of the Faith, "The Vatican Declaration on Sexual Ethics, 8, Origins 5 (1976), 489.

[23] National Conference of Catholic Bishops, "Pastoral Letter on Moral Values," Origins 6 (1976), 363.

[24] The Sacred Congregation for the Doctrine of Faith, "The Pastoral Care of Homosexual Persons," *Origins* 16 (1986), 3, repeated in the July 23, 1992 Statement from the Sacred Congregation for the Doctrine of the Faith, "Observations on Legislative Proposals Concerning Discrimination against Homosexual Persons," in *Origins* 22 (1992), 175.

[25] William H. Shannon, "A Response to Archbishop Quinn," in Jeannine Gramick and Pat Furey, *The Vatican and Homosexuality: Reactions to the 'Letter to the Bishops of the Catholic Church on the Pastoral Care of Homosexual Persons'"* (New York: Crossroad, 1988), 26.

[26] The Sacred Congregation for the Doctrine of the Faith July 23, 1992 Statement, *Ibid.*, 7, 176. This is a reiteration of the 1986 Letter, *Ibid.* 10, 381.

[27] Statement of the National Board of the Conference of Major Superiors of Men, August 29, 1992 (Silver Spring, MD: Conference of Major Superiors of Men). 27. Michael H. Crosby, *The Dysfunctional Church*, 107-108. The percentage figure came from *The Report of the Commission of Enquiry into the Sexual Abuse of Children by Members of the Clergy* (Winter Commission Report, St. John's, Newfoundland: Archdiocese of St. John's, 1990), 35-36. See also James G. Wolf, *Gay Priests* (San Francisco: Harper &Row, 1989).

[28] The Sacred Congregation for the Doctrine of Faith, "The Pastoral Care of Homosexual Persons," *Origins* 16 (1986), 3, repeated in the July 23, 1992 Statement from the Sacred Congregation for the Doctrine of the Faith, "Observations on Legislative Proposals Concerning Discrimination against Homosexual Persons," in *Origins* 22, (1992), 175.

[29] John Tierney, "Wrong Labels Inflame Fears in Sex Scandal," *The New York Times*, March 22, 2002. Rev. Donald B. Cozzens found similar findings from Vicars of Priests: "Our respective diocesan experience revealed that roughly 90% of priest abusers targeted teenage boys as their victims. Most priest abusers, we concluded, were not pedophiles in the strict sense of the term. They tended to be *ephebophiles*, adults whose sexual interest focused on post-pubescent teenagers, and in the case of the vast majority of priest offenders, on male teenagers," *The Changing Face of Priesthood* (Collegeville, MN: Liturgical Press, 2002), 124.

[30] Stephen J. Rossetti, "The Catholic Church and Child Sexual Abuse," *America* 186 (April 22, 2002), 11.

[31] During the second round of media attention in the United States to the issue of pedophilia, Pope John Paul II's official liaison with the media and a psychiatrist by training linked pedophilia with being gay. He also questioned whether homosexuals can be ordained validly, comparing the situation of a gay priest who many not realize he is gay to that of a gay man who marries a woman unaware of his orientation to men. See *The New York Times*, March 3, 2002.

[32] For more background on this (again realizing the paucity of data to support such anecdotal conclusions), see Michael Paulson and Thomas Farragher, "Priest Abuse Cases Focus on Adolescents," *The Boston Globe*, March 17, 2002.

[33] William Donohue, quoted in Dan Barry and Robin toner, "U.S. Catholics, Sad and Angry, Still Keeping Faith," *The New York Times*, March 24, 2002. Donohue scored the bishops for their "dereliction of duty." Richard McBrien wrote an article noting that the reaction of "the right" regarding the second wave of allegations of clergy abuse was a "widespread collapse of support for the hierarchy" which was previously unimaginable. See his "Rumbling on the Right," [Milwaukee] *Catholic Herald*, April 4, 2002. On the contrary,

Andrew Greeley opined that the sin of the bishops was that they had "excessive compassion for priest" who got in trouble even if it was "inappropriate compassion. One might almost say sinful compassion." Andrew M. Greeley, "Reappointment of Priest Pedophiles Stems from Sinful Compassion," [Chicago] *Daily Southtown*, February 24, 2002.

[34] Joseph J. Guido, "The Importance of Perspective," *America* (April 1, 2002), 23.

[35] *Catechism of the Catholic Church*, 1832 (New York: Catholic Book Publishing Company, 1994), 451.

[36] *Ibid.*, 915, 241.

[37] *Ibid.*, 1579, 395.

[38] *Ibid.*, 2359, 566.

[39] Fr. Richard McBrien, "Celibacy Is Part of the Problem: Pedophilia in Priesthood Signals Need for Systemic Change," [Milwaukee] *Catholic Herald*, March 21, 2002.

CHAPTER FOUR

Unhealthy Ways of Coping with Imposed Celibacy

Around the time I discovered there existed little scriptural foundation for my professed life of celibacy, I met a woman. Before her, I didn't have to confront the issue of celibacy. In fact, I even thought I had been dealing with celibacy in such a healthy way that I had published an article about it.[1] This new relationship presented me with my first sustained challenge to the "option" for celibacy I thought (until now) I had chosen freely. This relationship made me aware of how little I knew about celibacy and how unhealthy I had become as a celibate. It forced me to re-examine how I had lived as a professed celibate, how I would relate to her if I would remain celibate and whether I could live celibately in the future.

This chapter attempts to examine some unhealthy ways we often live as publicly proclaimed celibates. Some symptoms of the sick ways we express our celibacy involve asexuality and "careerism," intellectualization and disassociation, workaholism and perfectionism, repression and acting out, and--probably most frightening of all--a kind of codependency which can best be described the term of being a "pope's man."

Asexuality and "Careerism"

In asexuality one's sexual feelings and needs are not consciously admitted; consequently they will not get proper expression. Asexuality differs from arrested sexuality--which seems to be a key in understanding what led many priests in Canada and the United States to sexually abuse adolescents. Asexuality often occurs when we get so involved in achieving some other force than sex in our lives that our sex drive gets eclipsed. But, like all eclipses, it sooner or later gets overcome by some form of enlightenment.

I discovered a classic example of the consequences of asexuality while studying in Berkeley in the late 1980s. "Francis" had been in his congregation at least seven years. Previous to his arrival in Berkeley, Francis had studied for his doctorate in economics; his whole orientation had been geared toward the degree. Only after completing it could he move on to theology. Then he would be ordained.

When Francis achieved his goal of getting a doctorate, he came to Berkeley. There he experienced a new world of ideas and feelings. He became aware of sexual needs and desires in himself that had been long repressed. Free of his preoccupation with achieving something outside of himself–namely, the degree–Francis realized he had unresolved sexual issues related to intimacy that had gone unaddressed for many years. At the same time he began to feel a strong urge to get close to women and to experience sexual and genital intimacy.

As he experienced his own needs, he became more observant about how some of his peers were addressing their own sexual needs. He became aware of relationships among his confreres with whom he lived that opened his eyes to something else going on. He noticed some of the unhealthy ways a number of his peers were expressing sexual intimacy. Others were living as gay couples. He never before realized that so many men in his order were gay, especially at the seminary level.

He articulated his surprise to me one day in words that jolted me as well: "I used to just assume that almost everyone in the order was heterosexual and that gays were the exception. But since I've come here and reflected on what I've seen, I have changed; now I just assume the average seminarian I meet will be gay." Not long after, Francis left the order, started teaching at a university, met a woman there and was married.

Another form of asexuality can get expressed in a form of ladder-climbing called "careerism"--a kind of subordination of one's sex drive for that of power itself. The word "careerism" was used in 1999 by Cardinal Bernardin Gantin to describe his experience as head of the Curia's Congregation of Bishops. It characterizes the upwardly mobile ambitions among many bishops. Oftentimes that power is expressed in exercising influence over others in the form of control. It receives further reinforcement in patriarchal systems, such as the church. Herein any loss around intimacy gets compensated through various power relations. The personal loss of meaning arising from self-identification is compensated as one seeks to find meaning in the structures that under gird one's environment. What Jeff Hearn describes about men in the public eye, fits well the situations of priests and male religious who serve as public figures who suffer from careerism. One's sex drive not only gets ordered toward power; one's relationships with others with the same disease actually receives support rather than challenge. Unchecked, this leads to a system that actually finds the process and its dynamics representing a laudable goal. Hearn writes:

> The creation of more complex societies with more powerful public domain institutions provides the conditions for yet more powerful relations for men. Any possible feelings of "loss" for men--personal, existential, collective--may be more than "compensated" by new orders of men's power, both individual and collective. . . While the movement to the modern, and thence the postmodern, may involve loss, it also offers opportunities for men to gain power.[2]

A classic example of how asexuality can get expressed in ladder-climbing the steps of power in the Catholic hierarchy seems quite clear in a bishop I know. "Bishop Henry" finds his identity not in his person but in his role as bishop. Almost always he appears with his French cuffs and rabat. Everyone just knows that Henry wants to be addressed as "Bishop."

One time I gave input at a gathering of bishops and leaders of religious congregations. Since this assembly was an annual affair, relationships among the participants had become quite informal. This informality applied to their dress. No other bishop or priest-leader wore his "clerics" and all the women religious were in street clothes.

All went by their first names. Only "Henry" wore his official clerical garb. Everyone else (save his fellow bishops) continued to call him "Bishop."

Once during a discussion, one of the women provincials and he had a lively exchange. They disagreed strongly on the matter. Finally, the exasperated sister said some thing like, "But Bishop, how can you say something like that? You are a man!" Looking shocked at her challenge, and drawing himself up, he loudly protested: "I am not a man; I am a bishop!"

This man's identity was in his office, not in his person. Since then he has moved up the ranks to be an archbishop. Paradoxically, while he may have become an archbishop and may have notoriety in his own territory, when he goes to Rome, any significance soon begins to pale; others are higher on the ladder than he. He noted this situation at the workshop by bemoaning the fact that, when he goes to the Vatican and meets with the Curia, he is "just another archbishop." "They don't even pay attention to me; I'm nobody when I go there."

His feeling of insignificance in the face of the curial court was echoed in the remarks a Cardinal made to me. He bemoaned the fact that at least a dozen other cardinals were higher than he in Rome. And, when he came to the Curia, even he had to answer to minor curial officials.   .

I have known men who are priests and religious who have worked diligently to become bishops and congregational leaders. Sometimes their "career" drive for a hierarchical role has been palpable. I have experienced it happen at chapters in religious congregations. With one religious who became a bishop, you could just watch the ways he "schmoozed" with other power-brokering bishops in the church.

Intellectualization and Dissociation

In the "Francis" example above, his preoccupation with getting his degree kept his sexual needs from coming to the surface. Any conflicts he resolved in his head. In my own life, as I noted above, my ability to intellectualize on how I was being faithful as a "celibate" even found me publishing quite a good paper on the vow!

Intellectualization is a great way to avoid dealing with our feelings, especially those involving intimacy and sex. If I can keep everything at the level of facts, data, objectivity, truth and norms, I can avoid moving beyond my brain to other parts of myself and my body. By remaining at the head level, I can avoid dealing with issues of the heart and can stay in control. I have no need to become more defenseless, more open and much less vulnerable. However, such mind games can be played only for so long before a dose of reality moves in. I have discovered that Catholic celibates tend to be among the best at intellectualization and the most guarded about issues of intimacy.

A provincial I knew had to address deviant sexual and genital behavior by some men in his province. When I asked him how these celibates could justify their behavior, he said simply, "I just think they dissociate." Deeper forms of repression occur when we exclude from awareness those experiences and impulses that would be anxiety-provoking if they were consciously expressed. This is known as dissociation. It represents thoughts, feelings and actions that are incompatible with our self-concept or self-image. The phenomenon, highlighted by Harry Stack Sullivan, finds dissociation to be a defensive technique whereby thoughts and impulses which would threaten one's self image and which are expected by society are screened from consciousness. It distorts the reality of the thoughts, desires and behaviors that are incompatible with our perceived position in life.[3]

Workaholism and Perfectionism

Workaholism and perfectionism represent two more potentially debilitating ways we avoid issues around celibacy. A workaholic's identity revolves around what one does. A perfectionist's purpose gets linked with achievement. Such behaviors become noticed in a system that professes the need for priests to become holy and which honors holy achievements. In the interplay between institutions and individuals which reward unhealthy behaviors when true meaning is lacking, it is precisely these two dynamics which often characterize the priest who is considered holy, loyal and successful.

This can happen often these days when we face shrinking personnel in the ranks of the clergy and religious life. Those who remain are saddled with extra burdens. Sometimes in this nation a priest can be responsible for up to five and six parishes, to say nothing of the scores of communities individual priests must serve in developing nations. A friend of mine finally left the priesthood when he discovered he was burning himself out trying to cover two or three parishes every week. He felt a personal responsibility to bail out the bishop. Finally he realized the institution which honored him for doing this would just keep letting him do so until he broke. When it dawned on him that he was just being used to keep the system afloat, he left. The system would not change its way of thinking regarding celibate priests, with its consequent demands on him. So he changed his thinking and became free of its demands.

Perhaps more accurately, workaholism might be termed "work addiction." Work addiction better describes the true nature (as well as the devastating consequences) of this attitude, compulsivity and behavior. While some church leaders decry the lack of productivity among the members of their dioceses or congregations, I don't believe this to be the pattern. Studies show that the sixty-hour week for clergy can be quite normal.

Leonard Greenhalgh, of Dartmouth's Tuck Business School, has created a "taxonomy of workaholics." He finds in all individuals having a work addiction some deep form of avoidance of personal issues as well as an attraction toward the leaders at the corporate level in which they work. He writes that such a man "really strives to excel; he takes on challenges because he's looking for approval, particularly from higher management."[4]

In my own life, I've found that my work addiction often arose from feelings of fear. My fear had many faces: fear of intimacy which resulted in escape, fear of rejection which resulted in having to make things perfect, fear of losing control which made me do more things myself than I should and fear of being isolated and unaffirmed, making me want to succeed and be recognized by the power brokers in the organization.

Paradoxically, work addiction, supposedly embraced for "the greater honor and glory of God," often has little to do with God. Rather, it often has much more to do with the promotion of self for one's self-made gods and their ways. It usually has little to do with spirituality and self-transcendence. Such work addiction belies an inward emptiness under the mask of the holy. For instance, we create gods called "ministry," "availability" or "doing it right." These gods become the idols of our false or unfulfilled needs. Rather than serving the God revealed in Jesus Christ, our work becomes a false god in whom we (or our canonical superiors) are well pleased.

Perfectionism, a curse of the cleric, often relies more on performance than personality, on success instead of selfhood. A perfectionist's personal identity often rests in doing rather than being. A perfectionist becomes preoccupied with results rather than relationships. Indicators of perfectionism are low self-esteem and poor self-control, procrastination and fear of failure; it can include relationships that can be short-lived or troubled. Many times the tendency or manifestation toward perfectionism can reflect reaction formations against self-imposed taboos, including forbidden attractions and impulses, desires and drives.

Great differences exist between persons who strive for perfection in a self-actualized way and ones who continually seem oriented to ever higher levels of performance or some unreachable goal. The former have a healthy pursuit of some end that serves as a point of motivation. The latter are compulsive and relentless in their effort to do succeed; they also expect of others goals that can't be achieved. The perfectionist can never be perfect. Neither can anyone else.

Like workaholism, perfectionism often gets rewarded in organizations more preoccupied with performance than persons. "Making it" can replace meaning. "Doing it right" stands as a surrogate for right relationships. "Practice makes perfect" often means, "Do it my way." The "right way" can be "the only way."

Psychologists find that perfectionism is a common trait among children of dysfunctional families. With many people entering seminaries and religious life from dysfunctional families, the likelihood of having more who suffer from perfectionism in such environments cannot be far behind. A common attitude many of these perfectionists may have had as children--"If I get perfect enough, maybe Mommy or Daddy will help me"--often gets transferred to new ecclesiastical "father" figures. This dynamic, accompanied by external referencing, spells sure troubles in the long run for those driven by this obsessive need.

Another dimension of perfectionism with implications in a religious system can be found, I believe, in the way religious authorities have traditionally rewarded perfectionism with everything from perks to chancery positions and prelatures to sainthood. The effort to be accepted by such authorities and/or be befriended by them is often obsessive. Fear of displeasing them can lead one to an addictive form of perfectionism.

Repression and Acting Out

Repression involves an unconscious process whereby a person tries to keep from conscious awareness certain thoughts, feelings and experiences he or she is reluctant or fearful to face. Repression is synonymous with unconscious control. For one to be free or to consciously make choices is antithetical to the power of his or her unconscious processes. Not living under this freedom and seeking to repress it has a price. William F. Kraft has shown clearly the costs of such repression for celibate priests or religious:

> A person who categorically rejects a dynamic that is factually part of his or her make-up pays a price. Repression is a negative reinforcement; instead of expunging an experience, repression can increase its strength and promote pressure for expression. The ways a religious unconsciously copes with repressed sexual energy are usually not in the service of health. For instance, a sexually repressed religious may become frustrated, irritable, and angry. Or such a religious

may automatically abstain from intimacy for fear of being sexually activated, and he may use celibacy to rationalize such avoidance. Or a religious may project or displace his own feelings by blaming others for immodesty, or perhaps achieve some vicarious satisfaction and shaky self-reinforcement by becoming the community "sex censor."[5]

In dealing with repression, a significant difference exists between how men and women respond to situations where they have never truly and freely chosen celibacy, yet are publicly professed to be celibate. It seems that many women have some seminal sense or are conditioned in a way that enables them to sublimate celibately in a more healthy way than most men. I think that one of the reasons for this rests in the fact that women are socialized around relationships; men around sex.

What might represent sublimation for a woman can be repression for a man. While the relationship itself becomes the concern with women, sexuality and/or genitality itself becomes the opener for male relationships. Even the physiology of men sends sexual signals in a stronger and more immediately physical way than women. More than women, men usually feel physiological pressure to be sexually satisfied in a relationship, even though women seem to sense it more deeply when they experience it. Thus, psychologists say, many women find it easier to repress sexual feelings than men.

The easiest way people escape celibacy is to seek release from it through various forms of genital gratification or acting out. Masturbation is its most common expression. I find it almost the norm that, when priests and religious confess to masturbation, their rationale invariably involves some kind of loneliness or a sense of being misunderstood or unappreciated. Often it takes place to fill one's feelings of inner emptiness. William Kraft describes clinically what men know intuitively about masturbation—as well as other expressions of genital acting-out: the core motivation for the behavior rests in a deeply felt sense of deprivation, loneliness or hurt. Such persons "engage in genital activity to escape the pain of his or her lonely emptiness," he says. "Although this is humanly understandable, it is not healthy or good. When genital gratification is used to escape loneliness, there may be 'fulfillment,' but the fulfillment is only temporary."[6]

Genital gratification or acting-out also can also be found in many of the ways priests or religious spend their free time. Many know just what they will do sexually or genitally during leisure time, on days off or when they go on a vacation; often these revolve around getting sexual or genital release. I know of one bishop—who also was much discussed in the press for knowingly reassigning pedophile priests—who said at a meeting of priests in the diocese: "I know you are going to do what you feel you have to do; just don't do it around here."

Sometimes we act out privately and secretly; other times it is a matter of public knowledge. I once lived with a friar whom everyone knew went to pornographic movies on his day off. Others who are gay tell each other where cruising bars can be found in the nearest big city or where prostitutes congregate. For those returning from their outings, the code seems to be: "If you don't ask, I don't need to tell."

In one of the places where I lived in the late 80s, there were many seminaries. At various times the seminarians would have parties, mainly feted at the houses of the various religious orders. One of the new brothers at our house had been told for weeks to look forward to being invited into the party scene. When he finally did go, he discovered "twenty to thirty seminarians all over the place." In every room "something was going on." Wherever he went in the religious house he found at least some of the male seminarians kissing and embracing each other or some female guest. "I was given the distinct impression," he told me, "that, if I chose to remain, new levels would be available to me."

Being a "Pope's Man:" Ecclesiastical Codependency

Once, during my province's triennial chapter, at which we elect our leadership, I was in the final group of candidates being considered for provincial. At such gatherings, especially for the electing of our leaders, either the General Minister of the Order in

Rome or his delegate must be present. This is to make sure that order is preserved in the chapter's decisions. Given this necessity to preserve the well-being of the Order as well as of "the Church," the Roman delegate asked me to meet with him. He formed his two questions as to my qualifications for leadership in colloquialisms: "Are you swinging with any 'Suzie,'" and "Are you a 'Pope's Man'"? While today the delegate also might have to add the possibility of "swinging with Sammy," his second concern represents the critical issue in all leadership in the Roman Catholic Church. He himself was a careerist. He used his position at our headquarters to become a bishop and then an archbishop. He was forced to resign in 2001 due to allegations that he used his position to protect priests who were abusers in the archdiocese.

In the Roman Catholic Church, being known as a Pope's Man means that you have unquestioning loyalty to what is considered to be his or the "Vatican's" thinking and/or position on issues, whether they relate to matters internal to "the church" (i.e., governance and sexuality issues) or how the church is to relate to society (social justice issues).

In today's church nobody can be named a bishop unless "the Vatican" is clear on what the cleric thinks on such issues as birth control and abortion, married priests and women priests and gay sex. Furthermore, one must promise, in order to be a bishop in this church, never to publicly speak against "official" church teaching on these matters. This constitutes fidelity; it is demanded by oath. In turn, this fidelity and orthodoxy often get equated with sanctity. Holiness gets equated with submission to higher ecclesiastical authority,[7] even though church history shows that some of the greatest saints had continual friction with their ecclesiastical leaders.

One of my Capuchin confreres is such a bishop. I had done some work in Rome with him, so knew him enough to call him by his first name, even after he became a bishop. One day, after the Vatican reiterated the papal teaching on the non-ordination, I pressed him on how he could possibly agree. For each argument I proffered he simply said, "But, Mike, I agree with the Holy Father on this position." No matter how many times I asked "why," he could only say he agreed "with Rome."

In contemporary psychology, being a "Pope's Man" often describes being a classic codependent. Codependency gets expressed in various forms connected to "external referencing." Here one's identity is measured by the expectations of others. The "others" in this case can be either individual persons or institutional representatives. One's thinking, feeling and acting are effectively controlled by others perceived by that one as significant. Codependency can be expressed in a kind of mindless adherence to rules and rituals, as well as cultural norms and expectations. It also exists in older, career-type clergy and religious who have found their lives oriented toward upward mobility in the system which depends on being accepted by those in control. Given this, it is not surprising that a 1991 study showed Catholic laymen to be more independent than priests, and priests to be more codependent than laymen.[8]

In the late 1980s I became increasingly aware of how codependent I had become. I discovered that much of my self-identity revolved around other peoples' assumptions and expectations. My identity was not based in my own self; it was controlled by what others thought, felt or did vis-à-vis my "self." I was codependent to the degree that my identity and meaning were defined by these "others."

Unlike my Capuchin confrere whose "classic codependency" contributed to his becoming a bishop, it my case it was the opposite. I would not conform myself to their ideas and theology, their desires and wants, much less their expectations or norms for my behavior when I believed these to be contrary to the gospel or common sense. In fact, my way of being a "counter-codependent" expressed itself by reacting to these very things by thoughts, feelings and actions that were directly opposite. Nonetheless the ideas, desires and expectations of these others still controlled my own. While I acted against them; they still controlled me. In order to be free of this control, I entered a residential treatment program. I was surprised at how much anger it revealed I had developed as a reaction to what I perceived to be others' misuse of power.

Dominican priest-psychologist Joseph J. Guido wrote a fascinating and disturbing 1994 Harvard thesis on Catholic seminarians. His findings showed that three-fourths to five-sixths of the seminarians studied--who ranged in age from twenty-three to thirty-four--were not fully capable of self-generated meaning and values. Rather they derived a sense of self, meaning and values at least in part from the interpersonal and institutional contexts which constituted their environment.[9] While they may be similar to other men of their age in this culture, ninety-five percent of the seminarians studied were "not fully capable of constructing their experience and its meaning" at a level of personal integration and self-definition.[10]

Guido's thesis also revealed the high extent to which an adolescent level of consciousness still dominated in so many of these adult seminarians. He wrote that fully "one-fifth of these men may be relying upon mental capacities that more appropriately characterize late childhood and early adolescence than adulthood."[11] Furthermore he discovered that the overwhelming level of consciousness of almost all the seminarians was "inadequate to the challenges of adulthood." He concluded that healthy maturity for these men demanded that they "dis-embed" themselves from their present ways of thinking in a manner "commensurate to the demands and tasks and loves of adult life." If they do not, he determined, "they will increasingly experience a subjective sense of discomfort and an objective measure of inadequacy in the tasks they undertake."[12] Guido hypothesized that, in eight years or so after leaving such a controlled environment as the seminary, and left to their own resources to face these tasks, these (former) seminarians would experience deep crises as priests.[13]

It is to the ultimate crisis--the crisis of meaning itself–not only in mandatory celibacy in the Roman Church, but especially in the ecclesiastical system that demands it in order to keep people in control (and, therefore, codependent on the system) that I now turn.

Chapter Notes

[1] In 1983 I wrote an article that included reasons why I thought I was "still celibate." Not having had the experience of being that close to

a woman kept me from experiences that would have colored the way I wrote that article then. See Michael H. Crosby, "Celibacy as Fasting" *Spirituality Today* 35 (1983), esp. 236-37.

[2] Jeff Hearn, *Men in the Public Eye: The Construction and Deconstruction of Public Men and Public Patriarchies* (London and New York: Routledge, 1992), 59.

[3] Harry Stack Sullivan, "Conceptions of Modern Psychiatry," in *Collected Works* I (New York: W. W. Norton, 1955), 22-23.

[4] Leonard Greenhalgh, quoted in Walter Kiechel III, "Workaholics Anonymous," *Fortune* (August 14, 1989), 117.

[5] William F. Kraft, "Celibate Genitality" *Review for Religious* 36 (1977), 604-605.

[6] *Ibid.*, 608.

[7] The fidelity = orthodoxy = sanctity triad is at the heart of the neo-conservative vision/agenda for renewing the church, especially the priesthood and episcopacy. See George Weigel, *The Courage To Be Catholic: Crisis, Reform, and the Future of the Church* (New York: Basic Books, 2002), esp. 141, 230.

[8] Michael J. Doyle, *The Relationship o Cultural and Family Background in Dependency –Conflict and Need for Power among Alcoholic Roman Catholic Priests* (Berkeley, CA: California School of Professional Psychology, 1991).

[9] Joseph John Guido followed the taxonomy of Kegan, Broderick, Guido, Popp and Portnow which studied people in their thirties. They discovered five orders of consciousness ("epistemologies") which characterized people at various stages of development in this age group. *Schooling the Soul: The Psychological Nature and Function of God Images Among Roman Catholic Seminarians*. Thesis (Cambridge, MA: Harvard University School of Education, 1994),

42-43, 80-81.

[10] *Ibid.,* 78.

[11] *Ibid.,* 79.

[12] *Ibid.,* 44.

[13] Private conversations between the author and Guido.

CHAPTER FIVE

CELIBACY AND THE CRISIS OF MEANING
IN THE CHURCH

Over twenty-five years ago, I participated in a "think tank" on the future of religious life. Another attendee was Alan McCoy, O.F.M., then the president of the Conference of Major Superiors of Men. At one point Alan and I were discussing the phenomenon of witnessing many fine people leave our congregations. We agreed that the vast majority had left because of issues related to celibacy; most had contracted marriage.

During our musings, Alan said something I put in my mind's recesses until years later when I witnessed something else he had predicted that day: "If we thought we had an exodus before, wait until the next one takes place. The next one will not be a crisis related to celibacy; it will revolve around a crisis of faith itself."

Alan's words have proved to be prescient. Now, as more of our members continue to leave the priesthood and religious life, many no longer do so simply for reasons of celibacy. Although articulated in varying ways, a common sense revolves around the notion: "It doesn't mean anything any more." The system that once gave their lives and celibacy meaning no longer provides the impetus it once did. Why stay in something that no longer gives life, or may even stand opposed to your deepest understandings of the message of Jesus?

In the third chapter I quoted from a study of priests which compared the attitudes and behaviors of those defined as "legal celibates" and "personal celibates." The data from that study showed clearly that legal celibates had higher scores around the issue of meaninglessness ("anomie") than their peers who were personal celibates. Anomie results from unclarity, unrootedness or a vacuous sense related to something in which one formerly believed. One may find meaning in one's work--as seems to be the case with many older priests and religious today--but anomie relates to the living of one's life. There can be a great difference in priests who are satisfied with what they do but not with the way they are living.[1] This difference and dissonance is measured by scales defining one's anomie or sense of meaninglessness.

A fine articulation regarding the connection between personal faith and meaning comes from Sharon Parks, a developmental psychologist at Harvard. For her, meaning-making is an activity of faith. She writes:

> If we are to recover a more adequate understanding of human faith in the context of present cultural experience, we must be clear that when we use the word faith we are speaking of something quite other than belief in its dominant contemporary usage.
>
> Though faith has become a problematic [issue in our culture], the importance of "meaning" has not. Modern people can more easily recognize that the seeking and defending of meaning pervades all of human life.[2]

Meaning-making, according to Parks, involves the activity of seeking some kind of pattern, order, form and significance to one's life and one's surroundings. It represents the desire to make sense out of things and to discover fitting connections, especially in the surroundings where one finds himself or herself. She writes:

> It is in the activity of finding and being found by meaning that we as modern persons come closest to recognizing our participation in the life of faith. It is the activity of composing and being composed by meaning, then, that I invite the reader to associate with the word *faith*.[3]

Parks also makes a connection between faith and meaning and one's culture. For her, a culture involves the forms of life by which a people cultivate and maintain a sense of meaning. It represents that which gives shape and significance to their experience. This culture depends upon the ability of human beings "to learn and to transmit learning [regarding meaning] to succeeding generations."[4]

Prior to Vatican II, the Catholic culture (at least in my country, the United States of America) provided meaning for people willing to be celibate in order to minister in the church. It gave shape and significance to their experience. It offered particular rewards and nourishment for people like me as well who sought religious life. But those days represent the end of an era. Instead we find a more secular, less Catholic culture that still needs to make sense out of things, but will not find meaning in observing unchallengeable dictates of church authorities. This highly-educated generation no longer blindly accepts fiats from authority figures. Given this social climate, it should not be surprising that many people in such a culture increasingly find celibacy to be senseless and meaningless. They find untenable structures of authority which demand it but also feel powerless to do anything about it, especially when they realize they *are made powerless* to do anything about it as well.

When we examine the underlying dynamics that motivate many to take on celibacy–but not to embrace it--in order to be clerics, we find further forms of dysfunctionality beyond those mentioned in the previous chapter.

Consequences of the Crisis of Meaning Regarding Celibacy

When one feels empty of meaning, when one loses faith in a system previously accepted as life-giving or when one feels like an alien in a heretofore welcoming culture, a void is left at the core of one's self. In his *The Unheard Cry for Meaning,* Victor Frankl wrote that, even when neuroses could be removed from such a person, usually a vacuum was left. He calls this lack of meaning "the existential vacuum." He explained:

> The patient was beautifully adjusted and functioning, but meaning was missing. The patient had not been taken as a human being, that is to say, a being in steady search of meaning; and this search for meaning, which is so distinctive of man, had not been taken seriously at its face value, but was

seen as a mere rationalization of underlying unconscious psycho dynamics. It had been overlooked or forgotten that if a person has found the meaning sought for, he is prepared to suffer, to offer sacrifices, even, if need be, to give his life for the sake of it. Contrariwise, if there is no meaning he is inclined to take his life, and he is prepared to do so even if all his needs, to all appearances, have been satisfied.[5]

Frankl's insights about people without meaning who commit suicide make me wonder whether there might not be parallels with priests and others who can't find meaning in their sexuality (especially when it might be homosexual in orientation and, therefore, defined as "objectively disordered" by "the church") commit suicide. Certainly it seems to be the case with some priests accused of pedophilia.[6] Be this as it may, Frankl found our sense of personal alienation, meaninglessness or anomie can be detected in various symptoms. He calls the symptomatology of the existential vacuum "the mass neurotic triad." It involves depression, aggression and addiction.[7]

It does not take a degree in psychiatry, psychology or counseling to detect many resemblances of this "mass neurotic triad" among diocesan priests and members of religious orders today. However, by failing to challenge the meaningless "meaning system," people will continue to take on celibacy, only to find it failing as a viable option for them. Their consequent loss of meaning will then find many of them adapting by some of the forms noted in the previous chapter or entering one or the other forms of the mass neurotic triad. Meanwhile, the institutional dynamics which helped create the pathology in the first place will suffer more by having to find ways to meet the consequences of its failed norms in its members' psychological problems and/or aberrant ways.

1. *Depression*

The first symptom of lack of meaning that leads to the existential vacuum can be found in various forms of depression. One kind of depression refers to clinically defined depression. This represents a pathological mood disturbance that is accompanied by various thoughts, feelings and beliefs people have about themselves or their world. It is also can be found in the low-level depression that reveals itself in one's lack of enthusiasm, happiness and joy. It can have other manifestations that fall somewhere between clinical and low-level depression. Often these manifestations seem to have some links with sexuality (and celibacy) as Freud himself showed.

As a young priest, I first became conscious of the depression-celibacy connection and how my lack of integration could lead to dysfunctionality. I was assigned to an ethnically changing parish--from white to black--where many conflicts existed. Racism seemed everywhere. Increasingly I became aware of how whites exploited blacks. I was depressed at being part of the white race who did this. Within our parish friary we Capuchins also had developed conflicts among ourselves. Some friars wouldn't talk with one another. My depression deepened.

I coped by concentrating on my work. When done I would return to my room to sleep whenever I could. One night, however, I decided to go to the "Ad-Lib," a strip joint in downtown Milwaukee. I had never been to such a place before, so I didn't know quite what to expect. Inside the darkened room a few men sat at tables. Almost all of them, like me, were white. Most sat alone. Like them, I sat and watched the women on the stage take off their clothes while the music played. Most of the women were black. When I'd look around, I saw the men ogling the women who had become objects for their sexual satisfaction which they were releasing. Of course, they were paying to get their genital pleasure, even if was by themselves. For some reason this led me to think of the slave auctions. The more I thought about it, the more I realized that I was just part of this sexist, racist system that uses people and drops them when they can't perform. Then it dawned on me: by my presence I was a part of this. Now, even more depressed, I left. As the song goes, I was "looking for love in all the wrong places." I couldn't do what I needed to do--to find that love within myself and in relations of significance with others.

While the above story tells how I handled a depression that was deep, in conversations with bishops and superiors of religious congregations, I increasingly hear talk about another kind of depression. This is "low-level depression." It gets expressed in varied ways: low energy, low productivity, general feelings of being ill-at-ease and unhappy, a lack of spontaneity and feelings of futility. While some consider this phenomenon a kind of "burn-out," it reflects a deeper problem that too-often fails to get adequately addressed.

When enough members of a community witness such behaviors and a decline in morale, the tenor of the place takes on characteristics found in many residences which house senior citizens. In such places, the residents find no meaning in their lives. They have not accepted or embraced the inevitability of their approaching deaths in a way that might give them peace. So they feel condemned to a way of life they have not chosen. The resulting dynamics reveal a kind of "low-level depression" that characterizes the experience of people in places of death.

Once I lived with "Barry," a young man in temporary vows. As he neared the time to request permanent commitment, I found him more and more unsettled. His concern was not so much about making a celibate commitment that would limit his possibility of genital expression; his worry involved a deeper, communal dimension. This got expressed in a saying he repeated with growing frequency: "I don't want to grow old and live with a bunch of grouches." Barry's fear was not without foundation. It arose from simple observation. While he saw his share of happy, peaceful and involved Capuchin Franciscans living in our province, he also found enough "grouches" to make him worry what might happen to him.

One evening after he said again: "I don't want to live with a group of grouches," I asked him: "Why don't you be concrete so I can better understand what you mean? You must have concluded this from observing something happening in the province." As we talked, we decided to classify the attitudes and behavior of the twenty or thirty friars living in our Milwaukee communities as reflecting that of a "grouch" or a "grower." At the end, we shared our observations. Each of us, without sharing what we meant by the terms, had placed in the same categories all twenty or thirty friars!

Individual low-level depression gets compounded when the ecology of priesthood and religious life manifests a parallel depression infecting the group as a whole. While some would argue this seems less the case with diocesan priests,[8] it appears to be very much at the heart of problems facing religious congregations. Donna Markham has said that this "is suggestive of diminished morale and a kind of 'corporate depression' which is highly defended against through the use of denial and reaction formation."[9] Our individual low-level depression gets aggravated in an environment of institutional depression, especially when it is accompanied by institutional denial and/or the delusion that keeps saying this represents God's will.

2. *Aggression and Anger*

The second symptom of lack of meaning is aggression. As with depression, I believe connections can also be made with sexual deprivation or denial. The interconnectedness among deprivation, frustration, anger and aggression is clear to most everyone. When I was growing up people often talked about "frustrated bachelors" and "angry old maids." Instinctively, people connect someone's aggressive behavior or negativity with sexual deprivation. We even find ourselves saying of such people: "What they need is a good _____!"

The pattern of aggression is quite clear: some goal, need or desire is experienced. A barrier to those is encountered; this results in a sense of being deprived. The sense of deprivation creates frustration. The frustration triggers feelings of anger. The anger leads one to act out aggressively, especially toward the perceived source of the frustration or deprivation.

Some psychologists go so far as to say that deprivation always causes aggression and aggression is always grounded in some kind of deprivation. Regardless, where the two of them co-exist we will always experience frustration and anger.[10] Martin Pable, a fellow Capuchin and psychologist, finds one of the most manifest ways celibates exhibit aggressiveness and anger is in what he calls "low-key hostility." He writes:

In my experience, the most frequent syndrome I have found among priests and religious is what I would call a "low-key hostility." These are not angry people; they are quietly and passively resentful. They resent the burdens of celibacy, the ineptness of religious leadership, the confusion of theology, and the ingratitude of the faithful. Their prayer life--or lack of it--will often reveal that the low-key hostility is also directed at God; somehow he has let them down.[11]

Aggression (which differs from assertiveness) can be active or passive. When active it often expresses itself in outbursts or other manifestations of rage. Passive-aggressive behavior is often more controlling than active aggression. In institutional settings, where people feel they have no voice, passive-aggressive behaviors often exist, especially toward authority figures or toward those structures that represent unaccountable and autocratic authority such as the ones we find in some chanceries and, especially, in the Roman Curia.

In cases in which people and systems representing authority are linked with forces of control that result in an often (un)conscious sense of deprivation, a person's passive-aggressiveness is doubly hard to address. Psychologists have discovered that members of a group that have become accustomed to authoritarian leadership can often direct an aggressive stance toward a single victim. Other frequent manifestations of passive aggression occur in the undermining of others' effectiveness, jealousy and envy, as well as a tendency to sabotage common efforts and the subversion of projects. I knew of one leader in a religious congregation who would undermine any group agreement unless the idea had been generated from himself. He now is an archbishop.

Anger arises from a sense of being victimized by forces related to control or being deprived of experiences reflecting care. Like all emotions, anger can be used positively or negatively. It can be constructive or destructive. I've met priests and members of religious orders who have used their anger to challenge injustice in very creative ways. I know of others who have used it to control those around them. Repressed anger is another example. Its manifestations are often directed to and experienced by the people who are closest to us.

Many times, when people speak against a sense of perceived wrong arising from some injustice (such as the present dispensation related to celibacy), they themselves are defined by those wanting to maintain the status-quo as "the problem" and labeled as "disloyal." Or they are dismissed as being "angry." Meanwhile the authority in the system--that has betrayed the gospel understanding of justice (in the case of mandated celibacy) by demanding something unjust--goes unchallenged. This pattern also can produce a "blame the victim" mentality. The focus is placed on the "angry nun" instead of the abuse experienced by women in a patriarchal church. We wonder why "Father isn't happy," instead of seeing the problems of mandating celibacy as a requirement of ordination. We scapegoat gay people who desire to make a public commitment of their monogamous love. In this sense, Janet Malone's insights about the causes of anger in familial relationships make great sense:

> The sources of most of our anger arise out of relationships in which there is some type of intimacy and interdependence. We become angry with parents, partners, siblings, friends, and colleagues. Anger can arise in professional and social or church situations in which there is interdependence, or at times dependence, because of an unequal balance of power. Anger occurs when we have been hurt by significant others in our lives, whether personally, professionally, societally, or ecclesially.[12]

The anger generated by the experience of hurt or lack of care reflects not only a betrayal in relationships; increasingly, I find this betrayal also is closely connected to a loss of intimacy and interdependence. Many times the loss of intimacy gets idealized or intellectualized as a way of coping with the pain. However, in a significant insight connecting the loss of intimacy and betrayal of relationships with intimacy and interdependence, Carol Gilligan finds yet another element beyond the anger and rage that often flow from these feelings: depression, or what she calls "sadness."[13] While her notions are related more to women, the Dominican psychologist,

Joseph Guido, finds similar parallels among seminarians: "Like Gilligan's young women, these men are prone to idealize what they have lost and to rage against their sadness for what they want but cannot have."[14]

3. *Addiction*

Frankl's third leg of the "mass neurotic triad" stemming from a sense of meaninglessness is addiction. Elsewhere I have defined addiction as "any object or dynamic that controls, at any level, behavior, emotions, and thinking in such an obsessive-compulsive way that it leads to increasing powerlessness and unmanageability (at that level), and ultimately death."[15] These addictions find many priests and members of the consecrated life as well as homosexuals exhibiting attitudes and actions around substances, processes and relationships in numbers comparable with their lay or heterosexual counterparts. However, as with the other symptoms, individual addictions get compounded when the institution is addictive and remains in denial about its own and its members' addictive ways. The possibility of personal recovery is thus diminished since the addictions' presence and institutional reasons to sustain them are often denied in order to preserve the existing arrangements.

The most evident form of addiction, affecting the people considered in this book, refer to substances such as food, alcohol, nicotine, drugs and other chemicals, as well as pornography. As with the issue of celibacy, a denial by church leaders exists regarding problems related to addictions. In his study of alcoholism among the clergy, Joseph H. Fichter, stated: "There is a large difference of opinion, not only among the clergy alcoholics but also between them and church officials, on the current trend in clergy alcoholism. More of the alcoholics (31.3%) than of the church officials (9.8%) think that alcoholism is increasing among the clergy."[16]

Besides being addicted to objects, a second classification of addictions refers to what can be called "process addictions." These include gambling, shopping, working, exercise and even an activity like playing the stock market. I discovered the latter tendency in me when I oversaw some invested funds for another group. I was in California where I could get a "rush" two times a day. I could open the morning's *Wall Street Journal* to get the final reports from the day before. Then I could work myself up in anticipation of the afternoon's trading that was picked up in the *San Francisco Examiner*. The even more interesting thing about this was that, given my vow of poverty, the money wasn't even mine!

Some priests and religious have serious gambling addictions. This proved to be the case with one of our brothers; it had serious implications for our congregation. He admitted his problem but never sought help. Although they knew about his problem, the leaders did not demand that he get help until it was too late. His gambling with money found parallels in the way he gambled with the presence of the province's ministry in an Islamic country where he and some of our other brothers worked secretly. When he was discovered by that country's customs officers sneaking in religious articles, all his baggage was checked. This revealed detailed notes about the nature of the Capuchin mission there as well as the names of the men involved. He was placed under house arrest. Finally he and the other men had to leave the country. It was only when he returned that he was sent away for treatment for his disease.

A third form of addictive behavior that affects priests, religious and homosexuals in a significant way, I believe, deals with relationships, sexual dynamics and genital expressions. People can be "relationship addicts" in the way they use other people based on their utility. Others might be "sexual addicts," using people as objects for their sexual pleasure. Sex addicts are controlled by obsessive thoughts and feelings and compulsive, genitally-oriented behaviors with themselves or with others. While the tendency may exist for one or more of these forms in all of our lives, the problem arises when these forces take control in such a way that they undermine our integrity and commitments.

Because so many professionals in church ministry find identity in their roles and in what they do, their resulting inability to be intimate can easily result in unhealthy relationships where others get used and abused. This method of control can lead to a relationship addiction. I know of one priest who was expert at raising money, until his benefactors became savvy to his tactics: the only times they would receive letters or calls from him were connected to a request for monies for this project or that program he wanted to fund. When they needed something from him, he was not available. Sooner or later they grew tired of being used by him. His addiction undermined the effectiveness of the ministry itself.

Some relate to others in ways that feed unhealthy sexual addictions, even though they may never end up having genital sex. The expressions of sexual addiction have been described by Patrick Carnes, a pioneer in the study of this form of addiction:

> Sexual arousal becomes intensified. The addict's mood is altered as he or she enters the obsessive trance. The metabolic responses are like a rush through the body as adrenaline speeds up the body's functioning. The heart pounds as the addict focuses on his search object. Risk, danger, and even violence are the ultimate escalators. One can always increase the dosage of intoxication. Preoccupation effectively buries the personal pain of remorse or regret. The addict does not always have to act. Often just thinking about it brings relief.[17]

Whatever the sexual object of a person's preoccupation, when actions defined by that object dominate one's thoughts, feelings and deeds, the person is out of control. This can be true particularly in the area of sexual fantasizing and feelings of anxiety about whether or not to remain celibate. When such thoughts get expressed in behaviors, they can be myriad and destructive not only of self, but others as well.

Such is the case of a young religious I know. Given his good looks (and matching personality) women easily become infatuated with him. While his own sickness may or may not contribute to their own possible sexual addictions, his "drug of choice" centers on happily married women with children. At the point in the relationship where these wives and mothers let him know they are willing to violate their chastity and break their commitments to their husbands by having genital relations with him, he drops them.

Having led these women to "lust in their heart" fulfills his lust. While admitting he gets a rush in leading them on the way he does, he does not admit his behavior might be addictive. So his recovery is stymied. Meanwhile more lives get broken in the process. And he considers himself an excellent priest.

Another form of relationship addiction involves genital expression in various compulsive forms of behavior. These get expressed in masturbation, cruising, visiting pornographic book stores, massage parlors and gay baths. A growing phenomenon is the numbers of people, including priests, involved in Internet pornography. While writing this book, the F.B.I announced that at least two Catholic priests were among more than 89 people charged in "Operation Candyman," a nationwide crackdown on the spread of child pornography on the Internet.

Interestingly, in an insight that supports my thesis about control in the church hierarchy, Patrick Carnes includes in this group of addicts, people who are preoccupied by the need to repress their own or others' sexual and/or genital expressions.[18] I call this form of repression a kind of "sexual anorexia."[19] It represents the obsession of the "identified patient" in the institutional church family–namely, the clerical leadership–to maintain its supply: the preservation of the male, celibate, clerical caste.

Anne Wilson Schaef, herself an addictions specialist, writes: "I believe that many of our most outspoken leaders of organized religions are themselves sexual addicts. They are so obsessed with sex that they make it impossible for church members to learn about healthy sexuality in the church. Often, the church makes sex the most important aspect of a relationship."[20]

Another form of sexual addiction involves exhibitionism and voyeurism (or a combination of the two). The latter can be especially evident among formation directors, counselors and spiritual directors who probe their clients and directees for details regarding their sexual lives and experiences. Such voyeurism gives them vicarious satisfaction. They may never act out or invade another's body sexually or genitally, but they do so mentally and emotionally. This group of genital addicts includes those who indulge in sexually explicit phone calls, pornography or exhibit a pattern of consistent, unsolicited liberties with others, such as touching, patting or hugging.

A final form of addictive genital behaviors involves incest, child molestation, rape and pedophilia. However, when these forms of genital expression are perpetrated by priests and religious, they usually involve victims to whom they have related from a position of trust and, therefore, power. Their position of trust abused its power in some form of control. In almost all cases of pedophilia involving clergy and religious, the perpetrators were able to more easily escape critique and punishment because they occupied positions of power in ecclesiastical settings wherein their victims and their unsuspecting parents had first come to trust them.

According to Frederick S. Berlin, a consultant to the National Conference of Catholic Bishops Ad Hoc Committee on Sexual Abuse since its inception, the "two big concerns for society would be those who coercively impose themselves against adult women and those who force, persuade, or cajole children into sexual activity."[21] Both forms have been exposed in the second round of clergy sexual abuse here and abroad.

In various African countries the abuse of power has done yet-to-be admitted devastation. According to a report shared with "The Council of 16," a group of religious leaders in Rome, Sr. Marie McDonald, Head of the Missionaries of Our Lady of Africa, outlined the main causes of its expression in Africa under the title of "The Problem:"

> 1. Sexual harassment and even rape of sisters by priests and bishops is allegedly common. Sometimes, when a sister becomes pregnant, the priest insists that she have an abortion. The sister is usually dismissed from her congregation while the priest is often only moved to another parish–or sent for studies.
>
> 2. Many sisters become financially dependent upon priests who may ask for sexual favors in return.
>
> 3. Priests sometimes take advantage of spiritual direction and of the sacrament of Reconciliation to ask for sexual favors.[22]

Sister McDonald also noted that student sisters sent to Rome and elsewhere in Europe and North America often get sexually abused in those places. Such is their payment to priests and seminarians for help in their housing and studies abroad.

In looking for a cause for such abuse one need look no further than the culture which holds women to be "less than." In many countries women are educated to be inferior, to be subservient and obey–even younger brothers. Ecclesiastically, in asking why such aberrations were not investigated more thoroughly one need look no further than the episcopal culture of patriarchy that blamed the women for being abused or whose own members abused those who reported the violations.

Crisis of Meaning in the Institution

When relational, sexual or genital behaviors become addictive, one's personal and relational life becomes increasingly unmanageable. When institutions impose forms of control that can lead to such behaviors, life in the institution will become more problematic as well. Is there any wonder then, that data here and elsewhere shows people increasingly are having not only a lessening (if not a crisis) of faith in priests and male religious, but even more so, in institutional Catholicism as well?

Years ago, as I studied Frankl's "mass neurotic triad" that gets evoked in people when they cannot find meaning within themselves, it dawned on me that an even graver crisis is generated when one finds no meaning in the "culture of meaning" that should be being cultivated and experienced by its members. An individual's crisis of meaning (faith) becomes compounded when key institutions and, more importantly, the culture itself no longer generate or sustain meaning. Individuals and groups loose their faith in them.

I believe a strong link exists between peoples' personal crises of faith and an even deeper crisis of meaning experienced by many in our church today. Many are losing faith in structures that impose things like a male-only priesthood and mandated celibacy to the point that the structures themselves no longer mean what they used to. Thus the crisis of faith that once involved something quite personal has become institutionally-laden as well. In 2003 Bishop Francis Quinn said it clearly: "An overarching crisis in today's church is a crisis of faith, not in God, not faith in Jesus Christ, but a crisis of faith in the institutional church."[23] More trenchantly, Philip Sheldrake notes, the crisis goes beyond the institutional to the clerical culture: "What we confront is a crisis of meaning for an ecclesiastical culture that has depended on a complexity of symbols and on an ideology of separation and superiority."[24] Increasingly, uniquely for more educated Catholics, the present system just doesn't mean anything anymore. Literally, they find it incredible, unworthy of belief. The implications for those of us who remain in the institutional church (and who have not yet abdicated our own thought to the control of the Curia) can be profound.

The second wave of sexual abuse allegations has revealed this deeper crisis of meaning–not only in the institutional ways of abuse but, more significantly, in the clerical culture itself. It has been questioned as no longer able to provide meaning to more and more members, especially the more educated ones. A sign of this meaninglessness can be found in the 2003 Gallup poll that reported that Catholics attending church at least once a week declined from 39 percent to 28 percent in that year from the year before. The reason people gave for their absence that now exceeds that of U.S. Protestants? The sexual abuse crisis, Gallup said.[25]

Buzzards in the Sanctuary

A personally overwhelming and concrete sense of this loss of faith in the entire patriarchal structure occurred in my life some years ago when I visited Panama. My Capuchin brothers ministering there had asked me to give them reflections for a retreat. Three priests and one lay brother were ministering there in an area the size of Delaware. They counted nearly 40,000 people as parishioners. One priest must stay near the parish center in Chepo because his recurring back problems make it impossible for him to travel the Pan American Highway. In most places in this district it has been nothing but a dirt and stone road full of potholes. The other two priests divide the rest of the territory into areas with seventy to eighty chapels in each. Some of these local communities receive only one visit from a priest in a year. Meanwhile ministers of other Christian faiths are witnessing to Jesus Christ in ways that are winning over the hearts of many members of the parish.

My experience there evidenced a pattern that seems replicated throughout the universal church: although there may be dynamics defining a definite disassociation from the people by the institution's leaders, the real business of being church is taking place day after day at the local level. Although the people are lacking a regular experience of eucharist and the other sacraments, many lay ministries have tried to be as effective as they can. Many communities have "delegates of the word" and catechists. Young lay people called "missionaries" stay with the people for weeks at a time. These young people instruct and catechize. They prepare others for the sacraments which will be celebrated when the padre comes. The numbers and dedication of the lay people involved in different ministries is awesome. For two days, I observed a training course for over fifty, some of whom had walked days to get there. The theme was "discipleship;" the participants' eagerness and enthusiasm "to bring good news to the poor" was palpable.

After witnessing this style of church being promoted in Chepo, I was unprepared for another experience of the church in Panama: the installation of the new archbishop of Panama. The ritual, which occurred May 25, 1994, in Panama City stood in stark contrast with what I had recently witnessed.

In my Province, we priest friars do not concelebrate at Mass, so concelebration is not my experience. However I got the distinct impression that I'd be doing the friars a favor if I would join all the priests around the altar with the new archbishop. When I agreed I did not realize how much the ceremony would be a celebration of the male, clerical church. It was the closest thing to being at the Vatican for one of those Christmas Midnight Masses I've watched on television. As the ceremony progressed I realized it didn't matter where I was. I could have been in the Vatican or Panama City or anywhere else; I was part of a celebration of an exclusive, all-male club. The ritual installation could have taken place anywhere in the world. It just happened to be here. I was too.

None of us Capuchin friars had an experience like what would occur. We arrived an hour before services began. On the steps of the cathedral stood the new archbishop, José Dimas Cedeño. He was flanked by the apostolic nuncio, Archbishop Osvaldo Pailla. Both were in full crimson attire. Over their cassocks were beautiful lace surplices. On their heads they wore crimson birettas.

Soon more and more priests and deacons appeared on the steps. Next a large group of students from the major seminary arrived. (Not too long before at that seminary, some kind of sexual scandal had occurred. It allegedly involved some faculty and students. Those accused had been dismissed and the incident had been kept relatively quiet). Then more bishops came, some escorted by police. Inside, the cathedral was filled with many invited guest. Among these were the elite of Panama. Outside the beggars went about their business.

As I observed the scene, I found myself actually getting a very queasy stomach, so much so that I thought I might be getting sick. Never having participated in such a gathering of the triumphal, male, clerical church, and aware of my promise to participate, I felt ashamed about my complicity in something that no longer provided the meaning to me that it once had. I wanted to flee. Human respect and my disease of codependency instead found me submitting. I felt I could not go back on my promise to be part of the ritual.

As we were told to go into a back room to get dressed for the procession into the church, cars arrived carrying the Panamanian president, Guillermo Endara, and the president-elect, Ernesto Pérez Balladares. They were promptly escorted to the front rows of the cathedral. Members of the cabinet and the diplomatic corps already had been seated. It was politically important for them to be seen at the ceremony. Panama is a "Catholic country." Its leaders know the importance of keeping in the good graces of the church. The entire ceremony was being televised by all the Panamanian stations.

Two by two we clerics processed into the cathedral. Inside I found my seat near one of the side altars to the left of the main altar. Others higher in rank than me were more strategically placed nearer the main altar. Once in place, we spent the majority of the first hour listening to official proclamations related to the authority of the new archbishop. When the apostolic delegate from Rome spoke (for nearly twenty minutes) I kept waiting for him to say words like *Dios, Jesús,* or *Cristo*, which would give deeper purpose to the occasion. However, there was no mention of them. Only once did I hear him refer to *El Salvador* (" the Savior"). Instead, and with great frequency, other words were proclaimed and pronounced magisterially. These dealt with authority in the church, its source and its extension. Words for "archbishop," "bishop," and the "Holy See," and other parallel images dominated his talk. Though my Spanish is poor, I did not recognize much that would address the needs or the hopes of the people of Panama. All this led me to distraction; literally.

I discovered I was not alone. By now many eyes, including mine, had become transfixed on something else in the sanctuary besides the apostolic nuncio. High above the main altar and overlooking the nuncio, flying between the two domed areas, were two large buzzards. Unable to escape from their predicament, they would perch on one cornice for a while, look around, and then fly to another. Their perch led to many amused comments comparing their situation above to the occasion below. Somehow their presence and predicament seemed symbolic of the event better than any words coming from the nuncio's proclamations. It was clear to me: the image of buzzards in the sanctuary symbolized well what is happening with our triumphal, male, celibate clerical church.

As we clerics continue celebrating our rituals of arrival and entrance, of upward mobility and status, the buzzards hover as silent sentinels signaling the start of another story. Though our clerical carcass still may have some breath, efforts to provide life-support in its present state ultimately will prove futile. Though it is not yet dead, the buzzards have already begun to gather. Yet most clergy are failing to look up and recognize what is hovering beyond. We remain in denial about the death that must be endured for new life to come forth.

In concluding this chapter, I don't want to imply that the denial, dissociation and delusion of the institutional church leaders around issues of clerical pedophilia in the more-developed countries like Canada and the U.S., Ireland and Australia or the exploitation of women in Africa and other developing nations are unique to Catholicism. But what I do find to be unique is the way leadership in the Roman Catholic Church, at the highest levels of chanceries and curias, have used and continue to use all sorts of defense mechanisms to keep from addressing its death-dealing dynamics. Because of such abuse of power and privilege, they still may be posturing and may even yet enact rituals to celebrate its significance. But the presence of the buzzards indicates what lies ahead. Unfortunately, what they intuit by nature seems to lie beyond the grasp of those who keep the sanctuary for themselves.

Chapter Notes

[1] Recent studies of priests and religious which have discussed their level of satisfaction indicate a high degree of personal satisfaction with what they are doing and even indicate many would choose this way of life again. See Hoge & Wenger, Andrew Greeley and the *Los Angeles Times* studies. As indicated earlier, I am not going to discuss any studies in a way that would create a thesis, for I have discovered all can be interpreted in ways that really do not offer constructive directions to the crisis that is facing the structure and environment of celibacy in the Western Roman Church today.

[2] Sharon Parks, *The Critical Years: The Young Adult Search for a Faith to Live By* (San Francisco: Harper & Row, 1986), 12, 13-14.

[3] *Ibid.*, 14.

[4] *Ibid.*, 177.

[5] Victor Frankl, *The Unheard Cry for Meaning* (New York: Simon and Schuster Touchstone Books, 1978), 20. Frankl's words rang true to my experience as I wrote the above quote for this book in its first draft. A lay brother in a religious order who attended a workshop I

recently gave at a renewal program finished the program with a thirty-day retreat. The evening the retreat ended he took his life. He had just been accused of abusing a thirteen-year-old boy he picked up at a shopping mall near the retreat house.

[6] While writing this book, "a curate widely cherished in the local parish. . . committed suicide last week as he faced accusations in the Cleveland diocese's mushrooming scandal over sexually abusive priests." Francis X. Clines, "Its Bearings Shaken, a Parish Buries a Troubled Clergyman," *The New York Times*, April 10, 2002.

[7] Frankl, *Ibid.,* 26.

[8] See the conclusions from two studies of priests in Andrew M. Greeley, "A Sea of Paradoxes: Two Surveys of Priests," *America*, July 16,1994, 6-10.

[9] Donna Markham, O.P., PhD., "Religious Life and the Decline of Vocations in the USA: Reflections from a Psychological Perspective," April, 1987 (Silver Spring, MD: Leadership conference of Women Religious), 5.

[10] For more on this theory see Carol Tavris, *Anger: The Misunderstood Emotion* (New York: Simon & Schuster Touchstone Books, 1989),164.

[11] Martin Pable, O.F.M. Cap., "Psychology and Asceticism of Celibacy," *Review for Religious,* 34 (1975).

[12] Jane Malone, "Exploring Human Anger," *Human Development* 15 (1994), 34.

[13] Carol Gilligan, *Joining the Resistance: Psychology, Politics, Girls and Women* (Harvard University: Unpublished Manuscript, 1990), 17.

[14] Joseph John Guido, *Schooling the Soul: The Psychological Nature and Function of God Images among Roman Catholic Seminarians.*

Thesis (Cambridge, MA: Harvard University School of Education, 1994), 158.

[15] Michael H. Crosby, *The Dysfunctional Church: Addiction and Codependency in the Family of Catholicism* (Notre Dame, IN: Ave Maria, 1991), 29.

[16] Joseph H. Fichter, Ph.D., The Rehabilitation of Clergy Alcoholics: Ardent Spirits Subdued (New York/London: Human Sciences Press, 1982), 23.

[17] Patrick Carnes, Ph.D., *Out of the Shadows: Understanding Sexual Addiction* (Minneapolis: CompCare, 1983), 10.

[18] What Carnes calls "level one" addictions, I call "genital addictions."

[19] Crosby, *Ibid.,* 29.

[20] Anne Wilson Schaef, *Escape from Intimacy: Untangling the 'Love' Addictions: Sex, Romance, Relationship* (San Francisco: Harper & Row, 1989), 39.

[21] Frederick S. Berlin, M.D., Ph.D., "Interview" Regarding Clergy Sexual Abuse, Posted March 4, 2002.

[22] Marie McDonald, MSOLA, "Paper for The Council of '16:" "The Problem of the Sexual Abuse of African Religious in Africa and in Rome," in *The National Catholic Reporter* website: http://www.natchath.com/NCR_Online/documents/McDonaldAFR ICAreport.htm. Posted March 9, 2001.

[23] Francis A. Quinn, "A Looming Crisis of Faith," *America* 188 (April 7, 2003), 14.

[24] Philip Sheldrake, "Celibacy and Clerical Culture," *The Way Supplement* (1994), 26. Sheldrake gets support in a 1993-1994 study

of diocesan seminarians. The Dominican Joseph J. Guido writes: "In the first major study of seminarians after the close of the Council, the decision to withdraw from the seminary was most frequently associated with doubts about celibacy. While in more recent studies doubts about celibacy continue to be associated with a decision to withdraw from the seminary, the fact that such doubts are no longer of greatest importance and that doubts about a sense of call and felt religious experience suggests that more than demographics have changed since the close of the Council." See *Schooling the Soul: The Psychological Nature and Function of God Images among Roman Catholic Seminarians*. Thesis (Cambridge, MA: Harvard University School of Education, 1994), 14.

[25] George H. Gallup, quoted in "New Briefs," *America,* February 3, 2003, 6.

CHAPTER SIX

Beyond Abuse

To date the most comprehensive official, institutionally-sponsored examination of clerical pedophilia in the Roman Catholic Church that I have found has not originated in the United States. Rather it can be found in the 1992 Canadian *Report of the Archdiocesan Commission of Enquiry into the Sexual Abuse of Children by Members of the Catholic Clergy* (the "Winter Commission Report"). Besides examining allegations of pedophilia by a significant percentage of the priests of the Archdiocese of St. John's, Newfoundland, the Commission addressed "two fundamental questions about the series of events which occurred within the Archdiocese; what factors contributed to the sexual abuse of children by some members of the clergy, and why it took so long before the church became aware of the deviant behavior."[1]

As to the first question, factors of power abuse identified with dynamics in the institutional church "had a direct bearing on the occurrence of child abuse by priests of the Archdiocese." In Newfoundland clerical power had reached "a position of nearly absolute authority in everyday life."[2] Consequently, the victims were able to be codependentally controlled by abusing priests (and brothers).

The Commission insisted that this phenomenon could not be isolated from the clerical structure itself. It noted how a patriarchal (adult-male dominated) system had been reinforced by the authoritarian Roman Catholic church in that Province. Historically, as such attitudes became institutionalized in the policies and structures of church and society, they provided a strong, cultural and

133

social support for oppression. As a result, one person or group was able to dominate those without power.[3]

The Winter Commission Report demonstrated that the whole structural apparatus enabling this abuse was cultivated by five historic factors: the exalted position of the priest in the community, the Catholic school system which never adequately addressed the issue of sex, the absence of accountability at the institutional level, the patriarchal culture and the ineptness of the leaders themselves.

As to the second question--"why it took so long before the church became aware of the deviant behavior" (basically the same question that would be asked by the U.S. Bishops of their own situation a decade later)--the Winter Commission stated that, since the mid-1970s, Archdiocesan leadership knew about deviant and sexually inappropriate behavior among some Archdiocesan clergy long before the victims publicly disclosed that they actually had been abused as children.[4]

Allowing for rationales that would justify such silence, i.e., rightfully protecting privileged information, heading the list of reasons why silence became the rule for church officials was simply that they "denied the problems."[5] In the medical field, denial represents the normal response we make when a disease is revealed to be in us, especially when we tell ourselves we are healthy or such a revelation may indicate the beginning of our death. In a church structure defined by patriarchal clericalism, when the allegations of abuse attack the self-image of "health" or "integrity" that the leaders have applied to themselves, their organization and their operations, continued denial in the face of evident dysfunction often can result in severe self-destructive behaviors. Denying a disease often frustrates its effective treatment; unchallenged, its debilitating dynamics can facilitate the spread of the disease to the point of death.

Violence and Abuse Beyond the Domestic Household: The Ecclesiastical Household

In the same year the Winter Commission published its report on abuse by clergy which also acknowledged an abuse of power in the hierarchy (1992), the United States Catholic Bishops released a document entitled "When I Call for Help: Domestic Violence against Women." The bishops had been unable to agree on a pastoral letter on women for years. When they finally reached consensus the Vatican rejected their statement, giving them its own to approve. They did not accept it. The resulting document on domestic violence represented an effort to say something acceptable about women. The statement limits the bishops' reflections on violence to domestic violence, i.e., male-on-female violence. The document was updated and re-released a decade later (2002).

In both documents the bishops state that violence anywhere "is *never* justified." They declare: "Violence in any form–physical, sexual, psychological or verbal–is sinful;" and may often be a crime as well.[6] Virtually identifying violence with abuse (especially if one compares the 1992 and 2002 documents), they define abuse as any way one "uses to control another through fear and intimidation."[7]

This chapter represents my attempt to show that the violence and abuse that have been identified with priestly perpetrators reveal a deeper layer of violence and abuse endemic in the patriarchal clerical system within which these priests were able to function. Using the U.S. Bishops' statements on domestic violence, I will show that "violence in any form" must also include religious or ecclesiastical violence as well as bureaucratic and institutional violence. I will argue that the bishops' own definition of "abuse" as any way one uses "to control another through fear and intimidation" represents a key characteristic of their own way of exercising power. This way of control defines the power dynamics that can be found at every level of the patriarchal system of the Roman Catholic Church—from the local parish to the deepest levels of the existing hierarchical church, including the Vatican.

According to the bishops' letter on domestic violence, the heart of abuse involves control. Control is the negative use of power. Whether this power-as-control gets exercised in abusive and violent ways in the domestic home or in the ecclesiastical family matters little. Their consequence remains the same. Both leave their victims battered. Both forms can *"never* [be] justified;" both forms are sinful and may even be a crime as various grand juries have been showing.

Abuse, according to the bishops, involves a form of control that is maintained through fear and intimidation. From my own experience I know that anyone who speaks about this ecclesiastical violence does so in fear and intimidation. When a member of the clergy breaks the silence being demanded to ensure the survival of the existing norm regarding celibacy recriminations cannot be far behind. In one place a diocesan priest who speaks against compulsory celibacy is forced to recant; in another a speaker not seen to be supportive "of the magisterium" on this issue is dis-invited and, in still another, a vocal priest receives no assignment. In Pittsburgh, during the height of the 2002 clerical abuse allegations, a priest delivered "an impassioned Easter sermon on the need for reform in the Catholic Church;" he gets reassigned.[8] It is not surprising, then, that in many places many priests and church workers fear to speak out lest they lose their positions in the institution.

In their document, the bishops show how domestic abuse can be intergenerational. They explain that, when abuse gets passed from generation to generation, it can become accepted as normal, then the normal becomes normative. Normative values justify "why men batter," and "why women stay." When the normative becomes a norm in religion, there exist few alternative way of considering other perspectives.

After discussing how men abuse women, the bishops show how the scriptures have been used by men as a kind of norm justifying their abusive behaviors. These texts are well-known, particularly the "household" codes found in 1 Peter (2:18-3:7) and some of the Pauline letters (Col 3:18-4:6;1 Tm 2:1-8; Ti 2:1-10). Unaware of how such texts and others also can be used to reinforce patriarchal control in the ecclesiastical household, they reject they way the scriptures can be used to justify any form of abuse that constitutes the heart of control-defined relationships. They declare: "As a church, one of the most worrying aspects of the abuse practiced against women is the use of biblical texts, taken out of context, to support abusive behavior. Counselors report that both abused women and their batterers use Scripture passages to justify their behavior."[9] In even more powerful words in the 1992 document, the bishops declare: "As bishops, we condemn the use of the Bible to condone abusive behavior."

In another place the bishops discuss another issue regarding domestic violence that has bearings on the situation of ecclesiastical violence. They note how it "often is shrouded in silence" or secrecy.[10] Undoubtedly it is exactly such silence and secrecy that cloaked and covered up clergy abuse by bishops and major superiors of men-- from Australia to Africa, and from Europe to North America. With some of the shroud lifted, not the fear of scandal once used to justify it, but great anger on the part of the people in the pews and unrelenting reporters has resulted. And the silence still remains regarding the ongoing sexual abuse of adult women here and abroad.

When I finished reading the U.S. Bishops' 1992 document on "Domestic Violence" I called "Larry Franks." A few years before he had told me his wife divorced him because he abused her physically, emotionally and psychologically. Her filing for divorce became a wake-up call for his conversion. As part of his recovery, to help others in the same situation, he founded Batterers Anonymous in Milwaukee.

When we met I told him I had once thought I could understand some of the problems in the institutional church by applying family-systems theory and addiction theory. Indeed this insight had led to my then-recently published *The Dysfunctional Church: Addiction and Codependency in the Family of Catholicism.*[11] However, I said, in the bishops' own words about abuse in the domestic family, I had found incontrovertible parallels in the ecclesiastical family of Catholicism. Their insights had led me to conclude that my model of "addiction" to explain dysfunction in the church as an organizational family was inadequate and incomplete. "The deeper underlying issue," I said, "is that the males in the church, the hierarchy, have become abusers. Abuse pervades the whole system of control."

"That's exactly what we found out about ourselves," Larry replied. He proceeded to tell me that this insight led them to change their name from *Batterers Anonymous* to *Beyond Abuse*. "We still use the Twelve Step Program as the basic approach to our recovery," he told me, "but now we realize that our abusing arose from our need to use our power as a means of control. In the process we hurt ourselves and destroyed our families. I learned too late."

Unlike "Larry," I have concluded that, until our leaders can see the extent of the harm that has been created over the centuries by their abuse of power that has evoked fear and intimidation, they will never be able to make the necessary changes the current crisis demands. And, when they learn, it may be too late to change.

Even the most conservative of Catholic commentators have been loud in their call for change. "Of course the Church will survive, and more than survive, but I expect this storm is not going to pass any time soon. I expect we have not yet seen its full fury," Richard John Neuhaus wrote at the height of the crisis, in the April, 2002 issue of *First Things*. He continued: "I very much wish that I were more confident than I am that every bishop understands that there can now be no returning to business as usual. The word crisis is much overused, but this is a crisis."[12] While his prescription for their conversion is not the same as the one I will outline later in this chapter, he is quite correct in saying that something has to change if we are to be free of the sin that now binds us.

Given the crisis, for any changes to occur, it is well known that the abusers need to acknowledge it, admit the "exact nature" of their wrongdoing, and truly turn to that higher power, admit their wrongdoing and make an effort to reform their lives. Having done this they then can make a moral inventory of the wrongs that they have done, i.e., the abuse they have perpetrated, and make amends. Then they can begin acting differently, relating to others in a healthier way.

Applying this "Twelve Step" wisdom to the institutional church and its clerical leaders, until such a "program" is embraced, we can expect the abusive patterns to continue by its clerical members with consequent negative effects on the wider family. In the process they will be replicating in their own resistance to change the very dynamics exposed by Jesus regarding the religious leaders of his day who rejected his gospel call of conversion.

Unfortunately, like the highest governing council of the religious leaders of Jesus' day, today's Curia and its cardinals seem immune from self-critique. In a scathing op-ed piece in *The Wall Street Journal* Peggy Noonan notes that they

> have grown detached from life as it is suffered through by ordinary people. The princes of the church live as princes of the world. They live in great mansions in the heart of great cities, dine with senators and editors, and have grown worldly not in the best sense, in real sophistication and knowledge, but in the worst. They are surrounded by staff who serve them, drive them, answer their call. They are used to being obeyed.

The conservative columnist and staunch Catholic concludes that, while we "all suffer from some degree of arrogance. . . I have never seen star treatment ennoble the object of that treatment."[13]

While I cannot make such a scathing condemnation of our "princes of the church" (for I have known ones to be truly holy and helpful), it is clear that, as a body, they preside at the pinnacle of a power system answerable to nobody else. Paradoxically, this situation makes them suffer the negative consequences of canonically possessing (and, therefore, "normatively" being able to wield) unilateral power. Anyone questioning their authority will incur the response once given the layman Jesus of Nazareth. Who was he to question their authority and their way of exercising it?

Because I deeply believe parallels exist in our church today which Jesus confronted in his entrenched religious system, we need to return to the gospels to discover again how he challenged the "Tradition." It had become acculturated in religiously-sanctioned abuses related to power and sexual roles. Building on this context, I will show how our religious leaders also have used Scriptures and Tradition under the mantle of religion to perpetuate their power and sexual roles in equally abusive ways. I will show how this violates (i.e., does violence to) the core of Jesus' gospel about the inbreaking of God's reign or power. The chapter will conclude with a prescription for conversion and signs of reform that would indicate our church leaders are committed to a firm purpose of amendment.

How Jesus Confronted His Own Religious System Entrenched in Power and Sexual Roles

One of the best New Testament exegetes describing the cultural anthropology of Jesus' first century Mediterranean world is Bruce J. Malina. He notes that the dynamics that gave rise to Jesus' world of meaning revolved around notions of honor and shame. Honor and shame codes characterized all relationships of belonging. These codified how people were to fit in the social hierarchy. The resulting patterns were structured through three interlinking "boundary markers:" power, sexual status and religion.

For Malina *power* means "the ability to exercise control over the behavior of others," *sexual status* (or roles) "refers to the sets of duties and rights–what you ought to do and what others ought to do to or for you–that derive from symboling biological, sexual differentiation" and *religion* involves "the attitude and behavior one is expected to follow relative to those who control one's existence," ie., the religious leaders.[14]

Jesus, as the Messiah, exposed the way religion was being used to obstruct the reign of power of God in the existing power dynamics and sexual patterns of his day.

1. *Power*. While all gospels detail Jesus' confrontation with the powers-that-were, the first gospel stands as one extended account of Jesus' conflicts with the leaders of his day over power and the exercise of authority. His most significant opposition came from the very religious leaders whose *raison d'etre* involved waiting for the Christ to come so they could submmit to the reign or authority of that Messiah.

Matthew uniquely describes this conflict over Jesus' power and the religious leaders' resistance to it particularly in the ten ways he uses the Greek word *exousia* (power or, more specifically, authority).

The gospel's final words state: "All authority (*exousia*) in heaven and earth" had "been given to" Jesus (Mt. 28:18). This divinely-authorized power set him apart from the authority exercised in the empire, as attested by the centurion (Mt. 8:9). His teaching with *exousia* set him apart from the scribes of the people (Mt. 7:29) and his healing, combined with the power to forgive sins (Mt. 9:6) was defined by the religious leaders as blasphemous. The tension around the origin of Jesus' authority versus the exercise of authority of "the chief priests and the elders of the people" reached a critical peak in chapter 21. Herein and in four places, Matthew contrasts the *exousia* of Jesus with that of the religious leadership. They confronted Jesus over his authority "when he entered the temple." He then refused to tell them its source because they were not honest in the use of their authority (Mt. 21:23 [2x], 24, 27). Finally, because of the needs of the people, Jesus extended his *exousia* to "his twelve disciples" (Mt. 10:1) as well as those (Mt. 9:8) who would constitute his church (see 28:18).

The *exousia* given the apostles gets special specification with Peter's confession of faith (16:16). Peter's faith elicited from Matthew's Jesus the first use of the word "church" in the gospels. Even though we know that such words are neither in Mark or Luke and, therefore, not "dominical" but the redaction of the author,[15] they are part of divine revelation:

> Blessed are you, Simon son of Jonah! For flesh and blood has not revealed this to you, but my Father in heaven. And I tell you, you are Peter, and on this rock I will build my church, and the gates of Hades will not prevail against it. I will give you [*singular*] the keys of the kingdom of heaven, and whatever you [*singular*] bind on earth shall be bound in heaven, and whatever you [*singular*] loose on earth shall be loosed in heaven (16:17- 19).

This passage represents the theoretical context for what I call the *church of Matthew 16,* a model of authority expressed in the contemporary hierarchical church. It has evolved from a model that found power more balanced to one that became increasingly absolutized in Latin Rite Catholicism. Indeed, when the word "the church" is used today, it invariably means a "church" that is limited to the hierarchy.

It has never been stressed to Catholics that the *exousia* given the apostles that was specified in Peter's power to bind and loose also gets extended to the whole church in Matthew 18. The parallel passage describing what will be called the *church of Matthew 18* is found when Matthew's Jesus gives the same power to bind and loose to the church itself in 18:18: "Truly I tell *you* [*plural*], whatever you [*plural*] bind on earth will be bound in heaven, and whatever you [*plural*] loose on earth will be loosed in heaven."

Matthew 16:19 reinforces a hierarchical authority in the church (which is further reinforced with the granting of "the keys"), while 18:18 grounds binding and loosing in the collegial authority of the community (the two or three gathered in Jesus' name). Taking Matthew's gospel as a whole, it becomes clear that an evangelical exercise of authority in any church faithful to Christ cannot have its expression in 16:19 apart from its expression in the church of 18:18. Conversely, you cannot have authority in Matthew 18:18 divorced from that in Matthew 16:19. These passages have been parts of the Scripture from the beginning; Tradition cannot separate them now.

2. Sexual Status. Malina's second "boundary marker" defining belonging in the first century world involved the way relations between men and women were structured around the "oughts" of that culture.

As we consider how he dealt with sexual differentiation, it seems that Jesus was a child of his times. This is clear if we examine the first gospel's account of how he allowed/expected women to wait on him (Mt. 8:15; 26:6-13). Only one group--men--were his hand-picked coterie. In the case of the Samaritan woman who entered "his space" uninvited, he did to her what any self-respecting Jewish man would do to any other Samaritan (much less a woman): he shamed her by shunning her (Mt. 15:23).

Yet, even though he reflected dynamics found in his culture's honor/shame codes, other passages show that he broke or at least suspended the cultural codes that kept women alienated. Matthew's gospel makes this clear by including women in Jesus' heretofore all-male genealogy (Mt. 1:3, 5, 6, 16). Women followed him and shared in his ministry. In fact, it was two women who were told by Jesus to tell the "brothers to go to Galilee" to meet him in his risen form (Mt. 28:10). The resulting story shows that their witness was strong enough to make the men act on their words (Mt. 28:16).

Jesus' world was one where men were the only ones with value; women, like children, were discounted. They had no worth, with few, if any, rights. However, when it came time for them to share in the resources provided by Matthew's Jesus in situations where they did not count (Mt. 14:21; 15:38), they got equal to that of the men to the point that "all ate and were filled" even if they did not "count" (Mt. 14:20-21; see 15:37-38).

3. *Religion.* In the religious world of Jesus, the leaders' interpretation of the law and the prophets marked their way of controlling the people, Jesus stood in stark contrast to their interpretation with his understanding of religion as "justice or righteousness."[16] Thus, he told his disciples that, "unless your righteousness exceeds that of the scribes and Pharisees, you will never enter the kingdom of heaven" (Mt. 5:20).

The religion of the Jews of his day was oriented around observance of the teachings of the law and the prophets. As a religiously-observant Jew, Jesus said he came not "to abolish the law or the prophets" but "to fulfill" them (Mt. 5:17) even to the smallest part of their demand (Mt. 5:18). However, exposing how religious authorities can interpret such sources in ways that are not healthy, he also said that his approach to justice and righteousness went beyond that of the law-givers and those who claimed the cloak of the prophets (Mt. 5:20).

Jesus came to fulfill all justice in a way that turned upside down the religious leaders' codes dealing with the whole way the religion organized itself around torah and temple, table and territory.[17]

The resulting conflict between Jesus and the religious leaders over their exercise of authority vis-à-vis power, sexual status and religion came to a head with Jesus' diatribe against them in Matthew's chapter 23. Herein he labeled them with the most dishonorable name one could use of religious leaders: hypocrites (Mt.

23:13, 15, 23, 25, 27, 29; 24:51). While, before, he had called his religious opponents by this name (Mt. 6:2, 5; 7:5; 15:7; 22:18), his name-calling reached its apogee in chapter 23. The concluding words of the chapter make it clear that Jesus had concluded his co-religionists, led by the authorities, would not convert. Consequently they would be abandoned: "Jerusalem, Jerusalem, the city that kills the prophets and stones those who are sent to it! How often have I desired to gather your children together as a hen gathers her brood under her wings, and you were not willing! See, your house is left to you, desolate" (Mt. 23:37-39). Upon uttering this lament, Jesus left the temple, never to return.

Having reflected on how power, roles and religion were addressed by Jesus and now consider how they are expressed in the institutional Catholic Church today, it's important to note that Jesus' diatribe in Matthew 23 cannot be limited to "just a denunciation of Jewish leaders or Judaism; it is a warning to the entire Christian community." David Garland writes that it is: "a *didache*, a polemic against any religious abuse of authority."[18] Donald Senior, a member of the prestigious Pontifical Biblical Commission, also insists that "this list of indictments is not merely to pass judgment on past generations of Israel's leaders, but to scorch false leadership in the *Christian* community."[19]

Power, Sexual Roles and Religion in the Institutional Church

If power, sexual status and religion were the organizing dynamics marking boundaries in the first century Mediterranean world, can it be said that this same triad defines the underlying institutional dynamics in the Roman Catholic Church at this time? I think so. And I am not alone.

One needs only a skimming of the media, whether secular or religious to conclude that most conflicts in the church today center around power and sex. Indeed, in today's church, power has often become almost synonymous with sex insofar as canon law limits all authority in the church to *males* alone. In turn, these males make a promise or a vow *not to have sex* in order to function or have power in the church. This symbiotic relationship is hallowed with religious underpinnings and religious appeals.

At the highest level our religious leaders perpetuate their unilateral power by insisting it is God's will that only men professing or promising celibacy will have access to priestly power. Once given this power these clerics use their power to control how sex will be exercised by everyone else via their teachings around reproduction. The result finds sex subsumed as power through the apparatus of religion; all three organizing principles are sanctioned or made holy by God. It is God's will that such be the way the church is constituted and governed. All of this is ensured canonically in its laws.

Just as at Jesus' time, power, sexual roles and religion are still intertwined in the Roman Catholic church around deeply-embedded cultural codes of honor and shame. The next pages will detail how this gets done in ways that ensure the continuation of patriarchal clericalism in the church.

1. *Power in the Institutional Church.* Chapter one's review of church history shows how celibacy became the vehicle for the patriarchal institutionalization of power in the Church. Scripturally, where once there was a more balanced use of power between the church of Matthew 18 and that of Matthew 16 insofar as all elections of bishops were to involve the people and the people had the power to reject bishops they considered unworthy, power-as-control gradually got limited to the local clergy, then the bishops and now, at the highest level, it seems to exist almost unilaterally with the pope. This historical process of clericalization was accompanied by a parallel effort to clericalize all power in the church through priestly control and, ultimately, papal control that would be exercised through the curial apparatus which I detailed in chapter two.[20]

Today power has been so centralized and absolutized in the hierarchy that, even when the laity speak of "the church," they mean this group (as in "what does the church teach?"). In an even further concentration of this power at the top of the hierarchical ladder, in the papacy, Pope John Paul II has even referred to himself as "the church."[21] Such a statement makes me believe we are now witnessing the ultimate consequences of the prescient insight that Lord Acton proffered concerning the way he saw authority being (ab)used in the Roman Church, especially in the Vatican and the Curia by the Pope. After the First Vatican Council, which defined papal infallibility as a dogma of the Church, creating fear in all who would question the way its power might one day become unilaterally exercised, he penned his oft-quoted insight about power and its potential for abuse: "Power tends to corrupt and absolute power corrupts absolutely."[22]

With Pope John Paul II, the obsession about the prerogatives of the church of Matthew 16–to the actual exclusion of any authority in the church of Matthew 18–has turned 180 degrees from the theology and practice of the early church noted in chapter one. The current teaching has come to the point that he would say in February, 1990 that the "people of God is not the holder of the authority inherent in apostolic succession, as if the episcopal ministry constituted a form of popular delegation or is tied to this people in terms of duration or ways of acting." The ministry exercised by the bishops "is of divine origins," he added. "It does not need, therefore, to be ratified by anyone." Inverting this authority "runs the risk of subordinating, in a certain sense, the episcopal ministry, the faith and Christian life, into options made to the measure of humans."[23]

At this point it is important to identify the measure of the human problem that ensures and enshrines this abuse of authority in those who refuse to share it with the rest of the church. An examination of all the data related to priests here and abroad who have sexually abused minors indicates that it represents the average among other professionals: around two percent (although a thorough 2003 study by *The New York Times* put the figure closer to six or seven percent). If the former statistic be true, there exists no basis for allegations about "patterns" of priests being abusers, whether they are married or celibate, gay or straight. Whether it be two percent or seven percent, that each one was able to sexually abuse children precisely because of their power and celibate status is also very clear.

The data also makes it incontrovertibly clear that, with very few (but devastatingly serious) exceptions, the leaders among the almost two hundred (arch)dioceses in the Latin Rite of the U.S. Church (as well as religious communities of men) historically addressed the issue of pedophilia in ways that might be considered informed and satisfactory instead of self-serving and secretive.

With the resistance of bishops throughout the world to probe parallel sexual abuse of children and women, including nuns, and the pattern of Vatican officials to try to isolate such actions as examples of individual deviance, scapegoating the perpetrators or blaming a decadent culture, we must locate the actual abuse of power at its true source: in the aberration of authority exercised by the religious leaders in the institution itself. They exercised "their" power answerable to no others. Thus the Jesuit, James Keenan, wrote in *The Tablet* that the "molestation and raping of children" by individual priests were "not primarily sexual acts; they are violent acts of power." At the same time, however, he points to the deeper, systemic abuse of power by bishops and power, when he writes:

> When the bishops moved these priests around and assigned them to new parishes and let them have access again to children, these were not sexual acts, but acts of power.
>
> When the bishops and pastors denounced the parents and relatives who charged that priests had abused their children, these denunciations were acts, not of sex, but of power. When the cardinals tried to blame the media for unleashing a frenzy, these were not charges of sex, but of power.
>
> When Boston's Cardinal Law tried to issue a gag order to prevent the release of the records of one of our more notorious pedophiles, Paul Shanley, this was an act of power, not of sex. Similarly, when Cardinal Law's lawyers faulted a six-year-old boy and his family for not being more vigilant about Shanley, the issue was power, not sex. And when Cardinal Law recently told his priests not to work with an alliance of pastoral councils, his concerns were with power, not sex.[24]

After the first round of sexual abuse, almost every (arch)-diocese insisted (without independent verification) that it had installed procedures to keep such from occurring again. But, primarily because these were in-house procedures without transparency and external verification, we found ourselves as a church in the second round of abuse allegations in 2002, starting in Boston with the late Father John J. Geoghan. Again, with few exceptions, a pattern of institutional abuse and system-wide silence in the way they were generally addressed got exposed.

The abuse of power and governance by the religious leaders must now be addressed and radically reformed at its very core. This demands an honest examination of the way the Scriptures and Tradition have been abused to reinforce power in the church, sexual preference of males in power-roles in the church and the way religion has come to be used throughout the centuries to say such is actually God's will. Unfortunately, the patriarchal institution will not easily reform itself because it has come to interpret itself for centuries as a divinely-mandated culture of clerical privilege and power; this has enabled it to go virtually uncritiqued and unchallenged. Until now.

To preserve the patriarchal system, when a priest (who once was put forward by the people) is named bishop, it is so only after a full Curial examination has been made of his thinking, statements and activities. If he fits their norms regarding power issues and sexual roles in the Church, promises to defend the established patterns of patriarchal clericalism and agrees never to speak publicly against them, he is considered worthy to be honored as a bishop.

Inevitably, given his position in the church family, it becomes easy for a bishop to identify his own person with his role in the institutional church. I have shown how, for many if not most, this identification develops in such a way that, their personal identity gets subsumed in their function. As a result it is understandable why any criticism of the institution that has given them their identity (and meaning) is construed also as an attack on their persons. Thus they end up beyond critique. If any bishop begins to doubt some of the existing norms around power and sexual roles in the religion, he must remain silent if he is to remain in office.

When silence regarding abusive power and sexual roles is the pattern, dysfunctionality cannot be far behind. Sharon Wegsheider-Cruse shows that, when this occurs in a family, the system becomes closed, not open; it exists to meet a few key members' personal needs rather than all members' basic needs; its rules ensure the organization will be closed by reserving power only to a few in contrast to functional family rules that maximize all the members' potential.

In a dysfunctional family, roles become identified with persons, continually operating in rigid, anxious ways; functional family rules distinguish the role from the person, are invoked only when needed and then in a relaxed, flexible way. Using Wegsheider-Cruse's model, it becomes clear that, if we consider the church as a family, the former reveal the result of preserving the male, celibate, clerical model; the latter offers an image of what a more collegial community might be:

PAINFUL FAMILY SYSTEMS THAT LOWER SELF-WORTH	HEALTHY FAMILY SYSTEMS THAT BUILD SELF-WORTH
1. No-talk rule	1. Communication open
2. Feelings are internalized	2. Expression of feelings
3. Unspoken expectations	3. Explicit rules
4. Entangled relationships	4. Respect for individuality
5. Manipulation and control	5. Freedom highly valued
6. Chaotic value system	6. Consistent value system
7. Rigid attitudes	7. Open-mindedness
8. Reveres past traditions	8. Creates new traditions
9. Grim atmosphere	9. Pleasant atmosphere
10. Chronic illness	10. Healthy people
11. Dependent relationships	11. Independence, growth
12. Jealousy and suspicion	12. Trust and love[25]

If we would consider the institutional church from the perspective of a closed family system, we find the no-talk rule not only in case after case of pedophilia but throughout the system itself. Silence and secrecy characterize chancery and, especially, Curial transactions. In 1992, when the latter's Congregation of Education denied then-Archbishop Rembert Weakland an honorary doctorate from the Vatican-controlled School of Theology at the University of

Fribourg because he solicited women's views on abortion instead of only telling them "what the church teaches;" it didn't discuss its concerns with him.

The no-talk rule of secrecy gets extended into the decisions made among the body of bishops as well. Although a significant number of United States Catholic bishops disagree (privately) with the Vatican on its birth control stance, and while the overwhelming majority of Catholics disagree with that teaching, the U.S. Bishops' Conference in 1990 issued a statement on "Human Sexuality" reinforcing the traditional teaching. In the discussion on the text, Bishop Kenneth Untener of Saginaw, said that the bishops' failure to discuss any modifications to the traditional teaching made the church like a "dysfunctional family unable to talk about a problem that everyone knows is there."[26]

Besides the no-talk rule, a don't-feel rule prevails, especially when we consider sexuality. In family planning, the only allowable form of birth control can be practiced precisely at that time when women feel most inclined to have sex. For their part, priests are expected to keep their feelings to themselves or to sublimate them for the sake of the ministry, especially if those feelings are sexual and, even more, if those sexual feelings have a homosexual orientation. One of the most painful feelings facing people in ministry is the sense of loneliness, yet it rarely gets addressed. When people try to openly talk about issues of intimacy or when they are considered to be spending "too much" time with a specific individual, they are labeled deviant from the celibate norm.

Entangled relationships--in contrast to respect for each one's individuation--characterize closed family units. While most families find ways to deal with their eccentric characters, the institutional Catholic church cannot easily tolerate those who question its structural dynamics. Neither do its leaders listen dialogically to theologians whose insights are grounded in moral clarity rather than clerical prerogative. Oftentimes one does not know who is giving orders that end up affecting that one's future.

How manipulation and control rather than freedom and collaboration characterize the institutional church has already been discussed. The consistent value system with which many hierarchical leaders expect lock-step compliance often attributes as God's will matters that history shows resulted from quite human dynamics. At a 2003 conference at Yale on "Governance, Accountability and the Future of the Church," Bishop Donald Wuerl noted the need to distinguish between divine "givens" and human contingencies. While such a distinction is critical, what Bishop Wuerl noted as divine "givens" about specific forms of church governance, Peter Steinfels said as a respondent, can be open to challenge, based on a historical grounding in Scripture and Tradition.[27] We know this to be the case in the selective way the scriptures have been used to interpret the power to bind and loose in Matthew 16 to the exclusion of Matthew 18 and how this became enshrined in Tradition and Law itself.

Rigid attitudes often dominate any critique of the mind-set of the clerically oriented hierarchical leaders in the Catholic church. Many of these actually believe some of the disciplines regarding power and sexual roles in the church are "divine givens" even though a good course in exegesis and history would show their all-too-human origin. Rigidity is typical of any family where the no-talk rule dominates. In our ecclesiastical family, past traditions can be revered to the point that there seems to be an obsessive fear about creating new traditions lest people question the inherited structures of power, including infallibility. Probably the most striking case of this phenomenon can be found in the celebrated scenario around the decision by Pope Paul VI to maintain the teaching of the magisterium of "the church of Matthew 16" on birth control. Just over twenty percent of his hand-picked members agreed with the traditional teaching. Despite this overwhelming rejection of "official teaching," on July 29, 1968, *Humanae Vitae* reiterated the traditional stance on birth control.

In *Why You Can Disagree and Remain a Faithful Catholic*, the Benedictine, Philip Kaufman asked: "Why was this teaching so rigidly maintained?" He noted that members of the birth control commission "who insisted on the intrinsic evil of contraception conceded that they could not prove their position. Ultimately the real reason had little or nothing to do with reproduction. The decision was made to safeguard the magisterium, the teaching of two popes as recent as Pius XI and Pius XII."[28]

Another manifestation of a closed family can be found in an overly serious attitude toward life and a lack of humor among its leaders. On everyone of my infrequent visits to Rome, I am always struck by the seriousness and severity of the many clerics (and nuns) crossing St. Peter's square on their way to various Vatican offices. Although all their business is supposed to be of the Spirit, few I have seen seem to be exuding that fruit of the Spirit called joy!

2. *Sexual Roles in the Institutional Church.* According to Malina, the second organizing force that characterized social life in the gospel world of Jesus revolved around sexual roles, especially how women stood vis-à-vis men.

As I noted earlier, the bishops consider it abusive when the scriptures are used to justify violence against women. It seems they do so without realizing that, if violence is any use of power that inflicts injury, their own religious justification of a male, their insistence on a male-only, celibate-only priesthood stands critiqued as violent insofar as it keeps an ever-increasing number of Catholics from regularly celebrating the eucharist.

Almost two decades ago, the leader of a very large congregation of women religious wrote an article entitled: "Women Religious: The Battered Women in the Church." Her reflections arose from her experience as a major superior in the Roman Church. Certain officials in Rome had already undermined her authority because they did not agree with her collegial way of exercising authority. Out of fear, she would not allow her name to be used, lest she and her congregation receive further recriminations from Rome. Because fear and intimidation ruled her relationship with the Vatican, by the U.S. Bishops' own definition, she was abused by the Curia officials in the way they treated her and her order.

Another issue of potential abuse can be found among those women working in the ecclesiastical household. The very day of my writing the original draft of this chapter, I was told of a bishop who fired a friend of mine who was the Director of Religious Education in "his" diocese. He fired her with no warning, simply because "he did not like her style." In the family system called institutional Roman Catholicism, she has no recourse. Battered by her "church," this woman has no place for help or understanding, much less recourse. To whom can such a person appeal for redress?

Despite this injury done her, my friend not only wants to remain "in the house;" she wants to continue to work in that diocese. In this she seems little different from so many other battered women described by the U.S. Bishops in their document on domestic violence: she is "trapped in the abusive relationship" and has "no other means of support."[29]

While I have spent much time discussing the aberrant priests who have been abusers; they also are victims. They are victims of a system that imposes celibacy without proper contemporary supports. As a result those celibates who would not choose it were it not part of the "priestly package" often find themselves on different places on the celibate continuum. Sexual anorexics might be on end while sex and love addicts function on the other. It is hard enough not to be sexually anorexic when one embraces celibacy understood as a charism for service in the church; it is another thing to have it imposed by a hierarchy that can afford to be asexual because its members' identity and meaning needs not to come from relationships that are intimate and generative but from power and patriarchy.

Probing the prevailing cultural mentality dominant in the Roman Church often reveals more about the attitudes of its male perpetrators than their victims, especially when they are women. For instance, in 1989 a Vatican dialogue took place between thirty-five U.S. archbishops (chosen by Rome rather than selected by the National Council of Catholic Bishops) and twenty-five top Curia officials and Pope John Paul II. There several participants raised concerns about "radical feminists" who allegedly were refusing to accept papal and/or curial authority. Asked to describe "radical feminism," one cardinal, Antonio Innocenti, the then-Prefect of the Congregation for the Clergy, referred to those women seeking priesthood. "Their desire is fed more by a search for power than a search for service," this ranking curial member declared,[30] totally unaware of the possibility of his own projection on the matter.

In one sense the Cardinal was right: the issue of power is very much at stake when considering the clericalized priesthood in Catholicism today. In a patriarchal clerical way of thinking, men are able to have this power but not women; somehow only women seeking ordination are "seeking power" rather than service.

3. *Religion in the Institutional Church.* Some people have said that, because of the abuse of power evidenced in the second wave of clergy abuse scandals, an increasing breach of trust has occurred between the Church of Matthew 16 and the Church of Matthew 18. This would seem to be the case if we consider the fact that in one year, the people in the pews themselves seem to have instinctively differentiated between their local leaders in their parish priests and the top level of the bishops. In the previous chapter I referred to the 11 percent decline in the number of people who go to church on Sundays; however an even higher percentage involves those Catholics in the U.S. who are loosing trust in the bishops; it fell nearly 25 percentage points in the same period (2001-2002).[31] When it gets to core episcopal teachings regarding how power and sex are to be exercised, the chasm is even greater.

At one level there is less difference between the two "churches" than one would imagine. For instance, regarding institutional teachings of the church, among those Catholics of the church of Matthew 18 who actually participate in Mass at least weekly, 66 percent said euthanasia is morally wrong, 65 percent said rich nations should reduce debts owed to them by poor nations and 61 percent said homosexual behavior is against natural law. These percentages decrease in proportion to their regular participation in Mass. However, 100 percent of the church of Matthew 16 publicly agreed with such positions.

When we investigate other conflicted issues in the church, the differences are more stark (and become even more marked the less Catholics regularly participate in Mass): 53 percent of those regularly participating in liturgy said they disagreed with the church's ban on women priests and 54 percent disagree that Catholic priests should be unmarried; 61 percent disagreed about artificial birth control being immoral and 64 percent disagreed on the official teaching about divorced people who remarried not going to communion without an annulment. However, again, 100 percent of the church of Matthew 16 publicly agrees with such positions.[32]

Despite all the scandals revealing the abuse of power by the hierarchy represented in the church of Matthew 16, seldom have apologies been forthcoming. Belatedly one did come from Cardinal Bernard Law of Boston when he addressed the breach between the two churches. In the midst of parishioners calling for his resignation in 2002, he compared the situation "facing the Catholic Church in Boston and across the country to last year's Sept. 11 tragedy, a crisis which shocks the heart and soul and which must spark immediate and decisive changes . . ." Speaking of his own, as well as other church leaders' failings, he added: "Regrettably, I and many others have been late to recognize the inadequacy of past polices, the dimensions of the crisis and the changes required to restore a sense of trust."[33]

Despite all the teaching about the need for conversion in the church, only one document of the hundreds issued from the universal church of Matthew 16 implies a need for the "church" itself to convert in its institutional expression. This can be found in the Document on Justice from the 1971 Synod of Bishops. It states: "While the Church is bound to give witness to justice, she recognizes that anyone who ventures to speak to people about justice must first be just in their eyes. Hence we must undertake an examination of the modes of acting and of the possessions and life style found within the Church herself."[34] A similar recognition of the need for institutional conversion can be found in the pastoral letter on the economy by the U.S. Bishops. Outside of these statements, there has been no clear admission on the part of the hierarchy as a body that it needs to convert or change in any essential way. Without an admission of wrongdoing, much less an apology for it, we can only expect the abuse to continue—and to be justified as divinely-ordained.

I believe it is well-beyond the acceptable time for a thorough "examination of the modes of acting" that have created the dynamics that have allowed past abuses to occur over the centuries in the institutional church. As of this book's writing, even though there is nothing in the scriptures against women being ordained and because of the fact that the Pope has said the issue is not to be discussed, not one bishop in the United States who is head of a diocese has called for the ordination of women. The closest any bishop came to breaking the code of silence about the issue imposed by the Vatican came when Cardinal Roger Mahoney of Los Angeles said that such a question is "open" and my own (then) Archbishop, Rembert Weakland, said the issue should be discussed. However neither would state where they personally stood on the issue. Why? Fear and intimidation in the face of control..

Given the way authority in the Catholic Church has been almost absolutized in the Pope, the fact that he said April 21, 2002 that clerical celibacy was not open for discussion and that no bishop publicly questioned this, indicates the extent such autocratic power can be exercised unchallenged. At the very height of allegations about priestly sexual abuse, the Pope insisted to bishops visiting from Nigeria (where sexual abuse among the clergy vis-à-vis women seems almost endemic): "The value of celibacy as a complete gift of self to the Lord and his church must be carefully safeguarded."[35]

Fear and intimidation are the dynamics that still keep any real discussion about changing power and sexual roles from occurring. A key example can be found in events that took place subsequent to the appearance of an editorial in the Boston Archdiocese' paper entitled "Questions That Must Be Faced" in response to the crisis around pedophilia there. Four questions were raised by *The Pilot*: "Should celibacy continue to be a normative condition for the diocesan priesthood in the Western [Latin] Church," "If celibacy were optional, would there be fewer scandals of this nature in the priesthood?," "Does priesthood, in fact, attract a disproportionate number of men with a homosexual orientation?," and "Lastly, why are a substantial number of Catholics not convinced that an all-male priesthood was intended by Christ and is unchangeable?"[36] Almost immediately Cardinal Bernard Law distanced himself from "his" paper's queries. Within a week the paper issued an explanation, in effect saying that it was wrong to raise the questions.

But, even as church leaders fear speaking honestly about them and tell the rest of the church that they are not to be discussed, the questions will continue to be raised. We also can expect more revelations of more abuse. This abuse may not be as sexually-defined as in the past; however it will take other forms of control. Furthermore the violence that is structurally embedded in the institutional church through its clericalism and sexism will continue under the mantle of religion. Unfortunately such continued exposés of abuse may be the work of the Spirit in disguise. If the refusal to change is structural, perhaps only the Spirit will be able to bring about the end of the abuse and violence that now have been exposed but continue to be denied. In this sense, my hope for change rests in the insight proffered by Edward Schillebeeckx in his reflections on "Religion and Violence." For him christology and ecclesiology often have been captured by power interests that are controlled by historically-conditioned exigencies. If this is so, I believe that only an appeal to the Holy Spirit will be able to bring about the kind of conversion from violence that is needed if our religion is to be healed of its organizational sin. In this sense Schillebeeckkx writes:

> The actual historical violence of Christianity and its christology has its deepest roots in our continual forgetfulness of pneumatology. In it the redemption of Jesus becomes a historical and universal offer without any discrimination or virtual violence.
>
> Only pneumatology can prevent christology, too, from being violent. Without pneumatology any christology is false in a way that threatens human beings and is unorthodox.
>
> The actual historical violence of Christianity and its christology is most deeply rooted in our constant forgetfulness of pneumatology: the Logos of the pneuma blows where it wills.[37]

Can the Catholic Church Be Saved?

During Holy Week, 2002, at the height of the second round of abuse stories, *Time* published a Holy Week cover issue asking: "Can the Catholic Church Be Saved?" As I read the articles it became clear to me that the institutional arm of the Catholic Church cannot save itself until it recognizes the exact nature of its abusive ways, confesses its sins and submits to the Holy Spirit in whom there can be no distinctions around power and sexual differences. Until that happens we can no longer expect a "business" as usual approach to governance in the Church.

On Passion Sunday of that Holy Week something happened in a Catholic Church in Chevy Chase, Maryland that speaks to this point. *The New York Times* columnist, Maureen Dowd (admittedly no supporter of clerical celibacy), wrote about a sermon at Blessed Sacrament Church, preached by Father Percival D'Silva. He spoke about the good priests who were being tarnished by the abusing priests and the collusion of church leaders who turned blind eyes to it for so many years. At the end he challenged "the people in the pews to take back their church." According to Dowd, "At first the applause was soft. Then it swelled. Then people began rising in twos and threes. Finally there was a standing ovation."[38]

This standing ovation by those in a local community defined as "the church of Matthew 18," however, must be set in the context of another ovation in the form of the "thunderous applause" given the head of the U.S. Bishops conference in Washington in 2002 when he spoke to his fellow bishops representing "the church of Matthew 16." He said that some non-Catholics "hostile to the very principles and teachings of the church" were exploiting the scandal. Then he added: "Sadly, even among the baptized, there are those at extremes within the church who have chosen to exploit the vulnerability of the bishops in this moment to advance their own agenda."[39] Those in the Church of Matthew 18 calling for change around the power and sexual issues have "an agenda;" those in the Church of Matthew 16 intent on preserving "their" power don't, even though their past behavior has led to cries for reform in church governance.

With the peoples' cries for change going unheeded by the hierarchy, I return to the Statement on Domestic Violence by the U.S. Catholic Bishops. After rejecting the subtle ways abusers can use scriptures to justify their violence, they asked rhetorically in their 1992 document: "Can you imagine Jesus battering his church?"[40] In a non-rhetorical, very serious stance, this leads me to ask: "Can you imagine the Jesus of the gospels tolerating abuse in his church?" Unfortunately, when Matthew 16 acts like it has the "full authority" in heaven and earth to use the power given it by the Christ in a way that is unilateral and totally unconnected with that of Matthew 18, with sanctions for deviance that elicit fear and intimidation, its practices do make it a batterer, an abuser. Until it admits its wrongs, like any other addictive abuser, we can only expect more abuse to follow. It may not come in the same ways as in the past vis-a-vis priestly pedophilia, but it is bound to come—until the Spirit reclaims the Church for Jesus Christ.

A Modest Outline for Reclaiming An Ever-Renewing Roman Catholic Church

Some years ago I was asked to give a series of Lenten talks around the subject of my book, *The Dysfunctional Church: Addiction and Codependency in the Family of Catholicism*. Beforehand I met with members of the parish staff. Andy Katzenholtz was the young-adult minister. As we talked about the way power is exercised by so many in the Catholic hierarchy, Andy started getting very emotional. Then, with tears in his eyes, he said: "You know, the more I experience the things about which the bishops seem so concerned, and the more I look at the concerns of Jesus in the gospels, I don't know if I any longer can find Jesus Christ in the Catholic Church."

I am assuming that procedures regarding the reporting of pedophilia and care of the victims will sooner or later be set in place in every Catholic institution. These will force the leaders to be more accessible and transparent, open and accountable vis-a-vis any future aberrations related to priestly sexual infractions—at least in the developed nations around pedophilia. Whether anything similar will be done in developing nations around priestly abuse of women, including women religious, remains to be seen. Assuming this, I turn to the need for a new approach to the structure of the church itself.

The time is now for Spirit-led Catholics to reclaim the Roman Church for Jesus Christ. In an age of quantum physics wherein we know that life involves the overthrow of all matter and whatever separates rather than that which unites, we must change our hearts individually, communally and institutionally, overcome all the archaic and anachronistic and abusive forms of clerical power and, once again, allow the true reign (power) of God to define our way of being "church." Together priests and people at the local level, and both with the bishops at the diocesan level and all, with the pope and the curia at the highest level, must work together to become converted to God's reign, rather than the that power in the institution which has made itself felt in so many hurting ways.

When we consider how Jesus' proclamation of the gospel of God's reign set him against the institutional gospels of the imperial household and his own household of faith, we should not be surprised if we meet stiff resistance in our efforts. However, convinced that only a return to the Franciscan notion of the absolute primacy of Jesus Christ, in whom there can be no distinctions, will save the church from its sins of exclusivity in the form of clericalism and sexism, we can move ahead, assured of the Spirit's guidance. A first step in accomplishing this will come when we change our language.

It is sad to know that a basic reason why the Vatican insists on non-inclusive language has little to do with linguistic purity but much to do with male privilege. Yet, if we find problems here, a further challenge will come in changing traditional images used to promote and sustain the existing chasm between the clerical caste and the laity. We need to create a language about "church" not restricting its meaning to men or the hierarchy. We should stop using images like "children of the church" which implies we are a family of adults and infants.[41] Other images which may have had value at once, are now irrelevant. For instance, when we speak of "shepherds" and "sheep" we continue to make the leaders something entirely different from the laity; they are the informed ones, the sheep aren't quite human. Therefore they have nothing to offer. If we change our language we change our behavior. This leads me to the next step we need to take if we will find a church that will be changed.

Secondly, the recovery of the Catholic Church and its salvation will only begin with conversion—not only by this or that abusive priest but especially of this abusing system that has spiraled out of control. In his encyclical on ecumenism, *Ut Unum Sint*, Pope John Paul II said that Christian unity depends on becoming humble in the recognition of the need for conversion not only for personal sins "but also social sins, which is to say the sinful 'structures' themselves which have contributed and can still contribute to division and to the reinforcing of division."[42]

The media humbled our church leaders, in part, because that had become isolated and autocratic, answerable to no others. Even though these leaders have been chastened and have made changes in the way they deal with pedophiles, they show no sign of making any systemic change in the way they will exercise "their" power in a way that differs from the past. Until this happens, Stephen Rossetti, President of St. Luke Institute in Silver Spring, MD (which ministers to abusing priests) and a consultant to the U.S. Conference of Catholic Bishops' Ad Hoc Committee on Child Sexual Abuse, has written, the "media will continue to 'flog' us until we are duly humbled and chastened. It is a bitter lesson for us to learn."[43].

Thirdly, in contrast to its secretive ways, church leaders must create transparent structures at every level of the institution, not just those relating to pedophilia. This demands a new ecclesiology based on the dialogue which Pope Paul VI saw as a sine qua non in his encyclical *Ecclesiam Suam;* it also demands a new openness on the leaders' part to greater checks and balances that involve the laity in the basic governance of this church. In 2003 Bishop Francis Quinn wrote: "There is accumulating evidence that changes are needed in the operation of the church and in its exercise of authority."[44] This change must get expressed in a return to a governance structure based on the belief that "this church" is not the Pope nor the Curia's, neither is it the bishops' or the pastor's; it is Christ's church. All governance forms must arise from baptism and then orders, not the other way around. Noting the need "for an unconstrained acceptance of the promptings of the Holy Spirit,"[45] as Bishop Quinn concludes, demands that we return to ground church governance on the collaborative exercise of the charisms (including authority) rather than having all other charisms subsumed under clericalism.

Fourth, as I have insisted throughout this book, we need to find ways to collaborate at every level of the church to balance the power of the baptized in the church of Matthew 16 with the power of the keys in the church of Matthew 18. When we structure ways of governance that honor the uniqueness of each vis-à-vis the other, the whole church will better be able to serve the world into which it has been sent by the Risen One. We must not allow our challenges about balancing the power of binding and loosing in both groups, albeit honoring the keys as well, to force us into embarrassment when those intent on preserving only the power of Matthew 16 say we are "disloyal" to the Holy Father or otherwise heretical.

Fifth, to stop continued abuse by priests–be it of nuns in Africa or minors in the U.S.A. and Canada, Europe or Australia and New Zealand, or women and gays anywhere, the bishops everywhere must be willing to submit to experts the data they have regarding such abuse (as well as data related to other issues of the abuse of power and sexuality in the church). While, in the U.S., the National Review Board has begun making diocesan audits, the bishops need to overcome their fear of the findings and boldly work with the laity in ensuring ways to keep abuse from re-occurring once the facts are known and any patterns are discerned. In this they must be more willing to truly collaborate and learn from dioceses which have had programs that have actually worked over the past decade.

Sixthly, the whole church must re-appropriate its sacramental life to witness to the manifold forms of the real presence of the Risen Christ in the both the church of Matthew 16 and Matthew 18. Even a brief review of the ways the sacraments have evolved in the Latin Rite of the Roman Church show that they often have been developed in ways that have enhanced the control of the clerics. A case in point can be found in the action of the Vatican during the height of the U.S. pedophile crisis in 2002. It cracked down on "priests who had become too free in granting group absolution to sinners or otherwise become lax confessors."[46] Ways to celebrate the breaking of the bread and the forgiveness of sins must be honored and developed, promoted and celebrated beyond their unique expressions in transubstantiation and absolution that are limited to their expression only through a representative of the church of Matthew 16.

Seventh, at the level of the institution, the leaders need to begin an entire re-examination of the way power, sexual roles (of women and men, as well as gays and straights) and religion have been used in abusive ways that have hurt the body of Christ rather than helped it witness the gospel more credibly. Regarding the negative ways power has been used with justification in canon laws, a first step might occur with a re-examination of canon law and how it has effectively kept the laity from any participation in power–from the parish to the Curia. A critical but solid step regarding sex might involve reconsidering the church of Matthew 16's teaching on artificial birth control which has never been accepted by the church of Matthew 18 (and which, for many, began the breach in the former's credibility with the people in the pews). Finally, regarding Catholicism as a religion itself, a first step in its recovery might come when its leaders allow the Holy Spirit to become the ultimate authority rather than assuming full authority has been given to them with the Holy Spirit sanctioning their decrees.

Then, as a result of implementing the steps above, discussions might take place regarding how a healthy and authentic kind of celibacy will be able to be celebrated and honestly promoted as a truly free choice without any coercion. When this takes place, formation of both gays and straights as celibates can be implemented in ways that will make both effective ministers in the church and society. While the next chapter will try to show how this might be done, here I want to insist that, if we break the approach to celibacy that has made it a means of religious control of men over women and invite people to personally embrace it as a mandate of their hearts, we will have taken a giant step.

Chapter Notes

[1] *The Report of the Commission of Enquiry into the Sexual Abuse of Children by Members of the Clergy* (Winter Commission Report, St. John's, Newfoundland: Archdiocese of St. John's, 1990), 1.

[2] *Ibid.*, 13.

[3] *Ibid.*, 2.

[4] *Ibid.*

[5] *Ibid.*

[6] National Conference of Catholic Bishops' Committee on Women and Society and in the Church and Committee on Marriage and Family Life, "When I Call for Help: Domestic Violence against Women,"*Origins* 22 (November 5, 1992), 353. For the 2002 document see http://www.nccbuscc.org/bishops/help.htm.1.

[7] *Ibid.*, 355.

[8] Mark Berton, "Sermon Prompts Priest's Transfer," *Pittsburgh Tribune-Review*, April 9, 2002. In the defense of the Diocese, the priest did use a vulgar word to describe how he felt the people should react to the way the hierarchy had dealt with the issue of clergy abuse. According to the article, the priest, William Hausen, issued an apology saying he "in no way intended to confront the Magisterium of the Church."

[9] "When I Call for Help," *Ibid.*, 357.

[10] *Ibid.*

[11] Michael H. Crosby, *The Dysfunctional Church: Addiction and Codependency in the Family of Catholicism* (Notre Dame, IN: Ave Maria, 1991).

[12] Richard John Neuhaus, "Scandal Time," The Public Square, *First Things*, no. 122 (April, 2002), 62.

[13] Peggy Noonan, "The Pope Steps In," *The Wall Street Journal,* April 19, 2002.

[14] Bruce J. Malina, *The New Testament World: Insights from Cultural Anthropology* (Atlanta: John Knox, 1981), 26-27.

[15] "In what concerns the Gospels, fundamentalism does not take into account the development of the Gospel tradition, but naively confuses the final stage of this tradition (what the evangelists have written) with the initial (the words and deeds of the historical Jesus)." Pontifical Biblical Commission, "The Interpretation of the Bible in the Church," *Origins* 23 (1994), 510.

[16] Malina, *Ibid.*, 27.

[17] For more on Jesus' counter-code of holiness, see my "Matthew's Gospel: The Disciples' Call to Justice," in Wes Howard-Brook and Sharon H. Ringe, eds., *The New Testament–Introducing the Way of Discipleship* (Maryknoll, NY: Orbis, 2002), 25-35.

[18] David E. Garland, *The Intention of Matthew 23* (Leiden: E. J. Brill, 1979), 62.

[19] Donald Senior, *Invitation to Matthew* (Garden City, New York: Doubleday Image Books, 1977), 223. Emphasis is Senior's.

[20] For a discussion of the historical way power got centralized in the papacy (and by extension the clergy class), see my *The Dysfunctional Church,* 66-86.

[21] Pope John Paul II, quoted in Jane Perlez, "Pope Orders Nuns Out of Auschwitz," *The New York Times,* April 15, 1993.

[22] Lord John Acton, Letter to Mandell Creighton, 5 April, 1887, in H.A. MacDougall, *Lord Acton on Papal Power* (London: Sheed and Ward, 1973), 230.

[23] Pope John Paul II, Address to Brazilian Bishops, quoted in Catholic News Service Release, *Prairie Messenger,* Muenster, Saskatchewan, February 26, 1990.

[24] James Keenan, SJ, "Sex Abuse, Power Abuse, *The Tablet,* May 11, 2002.

[25] Sharon Wegscheider-Cruse, *Choice-Making for Co-dependents, Adult Children and Spirituality Seekers* (Pompano Beach, FL: Health Communications, 1985), 16.

[26] Bishop Kenneth Untener, quoted in John McCoy, "An Interview with Saginaw's Outspoken Bishop," *The [Seattle] Pilot*, June 18, 1992.

[27] Virginia T. Wilkinson, "Conference at Yale Explores Crisis in American Church," *The American Catholic*, May 2003, 8.

[28] Philip S. Kaufman, *Why You Can Disagree and Remain a Faithful Catholic* (Bloomington, IN: Meyer Stone Books, 1989), 70.

[29] "When I Call for Help," *Ibid.*, 356.

[30] Cardinal Antonio Innocenti, quoted in Melinda Henneberger, "Pope Orders Bishops to Investigate Accusations," *The New York Times*, April 21, 2002.

[31] LeMoyne/Zogby Poll, reported in "Bishops Approval Numbers Slip among U.S. Catholics," in *National Catholic Reporter*, May 23, 2003.

[32] "Contemporary Catholics: Who Are They, What Do They Believe," Zogby International 2001 Poll reported in [Milwaukee] *Catholic Herald*, January 10, 2002.

[33] Cardinal Bernard F. Law, Homily at Mass, April 21, 2002, quoted in Pam Belluck, "Besieged Cardinal Discusses 'Anger and Broken Trust,'" *The New York Times*, April 22, 2002.

[34] Synod of Bishops, "Justice in the World," 40, in Joseph Gremillion, *The Gospel of Peace and Justice: Catholic Social Teaching Since Pope John* (Maryknoll, NY: Orbis, 1976), 522. Only once, to my

knowledge, do the U.S. Bishops refer to the need for some kind of institutional conversion, but this deals with its economic activity. See their *Economic Justice for All*.

[35] Pope John Paul II, quoted in Melinda Henneberger, "Pope Orders Bishops to Investigate Accusations," *The New York Times*, April 21, 2002.

[36] Editorial: "Questions That Must Be Faced," *The Pilot*, March 15, 2002.

[37] Edward Schillebeeckx, "Religion and Violence," Documentation, trans. John Bowden, in Wim Beuken and Karl-Josef Kuschel, eds., *Religion as a Source of Violence*, Concilium (London: SCM and Maryknoll, NY: Orbis, 1997), 142.

[38] Maureen Dowd, quoting Rev. Percival D'Silva, "Rome Fiddles, We Burn," *The New York Times*, March 27, 2002.

[39] Bishop Wilton Gregory, Address to U.S. Conference of Catholic Bishops, November, 2002, quoted in Kevin Clarke, "Whitewash Renewal?," *U.S. Catholic*, June, 2003, 14.

[40] "When I Call for Help," *Ibid.*, 357.

[41] The notion of "children" of the church was often by Pope John Paul in describing aberrant behavior toward others for which he apologized. Never does he note that the ones perpetrating the crimes in the name of the church and with its institutional backing were members of the hierarchy.

[42] Pope John Paul II, *Ut Unum Sint*, 34, *Origins* 25 (1995), 57.

[43] Stephen J. Rossetti, "The Catholic Church and Child Sexual Abuse," *America* 186 (April 22, 2002), 15.

[44] Francis A. Quinn, "A Looming Crisis of Faith," *America* 188 (April 7, 2003), 15.

[45] *Ibid.*, 16.

[46] Melinda Henneberger, "Priests Told to Cut Back on Absolution for Groups," *The New York Times*, May 3, 2002.

CHAPTER SEVEN

Intimacy: The Only Healthy Way to Live Celibately

Some years ago, Fred Hickey, a young man interested in joining my province of Capuchin Franciscans, came to live with us in Milwaukee. Not too long after Fred came into the room where I was sitting. "Mike, I've got something to tell you," he began. "I've really tried to connect with the Capuchins and like you guys, but I've become convinced I just can't do it. I know I've got to be married someday."

My first reaction was selfish: again we would be losing another fine candidate. But, since he had offered the best reason why he shouldn't be in a group like ours that professes celibacy, I agreed that his rationale for leaving made sense. His response, however, led me to wonder to myself whether a celibate group like ours really had a future if it would not be part of the control dynamics presently in the church. So I asked him: "Fred, do you think there's any room for celibacy in the future church?"

Fred's response was immediate, clear and emphatic: "Oh sure!"

"Well, then," I queried further, "if celibacy has a place in the future, what will it take for someone really to be celibate?"

Without a moment's hesitation, this twenty-nine-year-old offered one of the best definitions of healthy celibacy I have ever heard: "Well, if people really are going to be celibate, they are going to have to find ways of becoming warm and intimate with others, and also to have a place in their hearts only for God."

As I consider the problems with pedophilia that have raised concerns about mandatory celibacy (though no causal link between the two can be made) and the deeper, systemic problems associated with those who insist on its maintenance, Fred's insight seems more apropos than ever. Although his articulation assumed genital abstinence, Fred's definition has become core to my understanding of celibacy: *the embrace of a divinely offered gift inviting one to freely choose a life-commitment of abstention from genital intimacy which expresses itself in an alternate intimacy with God and others.*

From Fred's words, it is clear that the only viable option for a truly healthy form of celibacy involves warmth and intimacy with some others; it also demands that we maintain a place in our heart just for God. While such may be the same recipe for health in any person of faith, it is mandatory that those who are celibates will be centered around these two poles.

Over the years, Fred's response has led me to recall unhealthy ways I have expressed my own celibacy. It also made me think of how others have coped with theirs. Not one of the "options" discussed in chapters four and five represents a viable, healthy way of living the celibate life. None represent a way of becoming warm and intimate. On the contrary, they actually represent defenses which keep us from being intimate. Not one invites people to have a place in their heart only for God. Yet, too often, these coping mechanisms and ways of reacting to what is becoming more and more meaningless (especially in the diocesan priesthood) characterize the style of celibate living that too many have accepted. While these options may not have done permanent damage to some of us, oftentimes they have been powerful enough for us to do harm to others.

In the second round of sex abuse by priests, we have found ourselves asking questions, as never before, about the institutional church which demands celibacy of its leaders. It has demanded it because its hierarchy has not been able to free itself from the existing model of the church and rethink what leadership in the church might look like without celibacy as a constituent of being a priest.

As this chapter develops Fred's notion of celibacy around its horizontal dimension (warmth and intimacy with others) and its vertical direction (toward God alone) it should become abundantly clear that a serious "rethinking of celibacy" will demand a restructuring of the church if it will be reclaimed for Christ. Because the bishops cannot imagine a church free of their unilateral control, it just may be such a rethinking of celibacy around intimacy may represent a first step in freeing the institutional church from its dysfunctional mindset about sex itself that has come to enslave it. Unfortunately, just as I believe the leaders cannot imagine a church free of their control, the evidence shows that neither can they envision a church defined by another approach to celibacy, much less sexuality itself.

Celibacy as Fasting

A metaphor that helps me understand the problems and potential of celibacy is to view it as fasting. The fast required of a healthy celibate must involve three interrelated elements: a fasting *from* (abstinence), a fasting *for* (healthy motivation) and a fasting *with* (the need to be supported in the fasting). All must be integrated. If I limit my fasting to abstention I can easily become sexually anorexic. If I live in an institution obsessed with preserving mandated celibacy I will live among sexually anorexics. If I limit my fasting to what I am fasting for, and this "for" is grounded in reasons outside my "I am," sooner or later problems will develop. If I live in an institution that tries to tell me that my fasting is "for" functional reasons such as better ministry, more availability or more effective witness, these motivations will not be sufficient when the fasting "from" becomes dominant. If I am fasting "with" and have no referent beyond just living with others regarding something so personal, sooner or later, my personal need for self-definition and intimacy will come to the fore. And if I live in an institution which organizationally seems unable to comprehend what healthy intimacy demands of its celibates, I will not be able to get help from the very ones whom that institution's leaders say must model authentic celibacy within a life-giving atmosphere.

1. *Celibacy as Fasting From*: Unfortunately, too often, when celibacy is mandated--be it for priests or gays--the stress too often gets limited to "not having sex." When this occurs, as in any other

kind of denial of that which gives pleasure, anorexia often results. Just as an overstress on fasting from food (as on some days during Lent) can make one hungry, an overstress on fasting from sex can make one a sexual anorexic.

My experience teaches me that, when sexual anorexics become leaders in the church curias, in dioceses or in our congregations, issues around celibacy cannot be addressed , on the one hand, with commands like "don't," "can't," "not allowed," "mustn't," or "shouldn't." On the other hand, when aberrations occur among the rank-and-file (such as abusive priests acting out), the refusal of the institutional leaders to acknowledge even the possibility of addressing problems connected to mandatory celibacy shows an even deeper sexual anorexia on their part.

When the emphasis in this core area of our life is "not having sex," it often also means "not having intimacy." I joined the Midwest Capuchins when I was nineteen. My class of thirty-one novices ranged from seventeen to twenty-three. I was one of the few who had gone to a co-ed high school; most came from secondary level seminaries. One of my class, who later left the Order to become a diocesan priest, is now serving time for repeated abuse of adolescent boys. Most of my class have left—for reasons of celibacy.

One of the first things taught was to avoid "particular friendships;" an ill-chosen phrase of that time used to keep close friendships from going awry. I learned it from a novice master who not only invaded our sexual boundaries by his voyeurism but, by such instruction, sabotaged any healthy way we might learn how to relate intimately to each other.

In novitiate, I knew I had a special attraction to Frater Linus. I first met him when I came to the college seminary after high school. Knowing he would be in the novitiate class, I looked forward to the chance of becoming friends. How wrong I was! Almost immediately, from the novice master's talks and conferences, I was led to believe that there was something very wrong with having any kind of attraction to another man. Furthermore, if I'd choose to spend time with him, rather than some others, I could easily be headed toward a "particular friendship." Fearful of cutting my budding "celibacy," I never allowed myself to get close to Linus.

I did not know my attraction to Linus was something God-given to me as a sexual being. Neither did I learn then that all authentic friendships must be particular. The only thing that makes something potentially dangerous or destructive for a celibate is not when a friendship is particular, but when it becomes exclusive.

The institutional preoccupation with "PFs" as they were called then actually undermined the possibility of candidates in the seminary and religious life developing authentic forms of intimacy. As a result many of us developed what Erik Erikson called the counterpoint of intimacy: "distantiation." In plain words this meant "keeping your distance." Erikson defined it as "the readiness to isolate and, if necessary, to destroy those forces and people whose essence seems dangerous to one's own, and whose 'territory' seems to encroach on the extent of one's intimate relations."[1]

In today's more promiscuous society, at least in Western Europe and North America, intimacy too often gets identified with genitality or the pursuit of some kind of illicit sexual pleasure. If someone asks another after spending time with a friend: "Were you intimate?," it often means: "Did you have sex?" In our overly-sexed culture, intimacy often gets equated with orgasm rather than relationships.

How did all this conflation of intimacy and genitality begin? Maybe it started when clothes covering women's genitals got called "intimate apparel." Maybe it received reinforcement when perfumes were given names dealing with obsession, seduction or conquest that is genital. Who really knows how they got equated? Whatever; intimacy has been conflated in our culture with genital intercourse.

Surprisingly, despite all the official teaching of the Catholic Church against pre-marital genital intercourse or demands that one *fast from* genital sex, the recent increase numbers of young people making commitments voluntarily to remain celibate until marriage has not come from Catholic sources. It has been arisen from other Christian denominations, especially Southern Baptists. Increasingly, virginity and abstinence, chastity and celibacy are being freely embraced under the motto: "True Love Waits." Data shows the pledge is quite effective.[2] Similarly, efforts among adults to create support systems for celibacy are not originating in the Catholic Church but in chat rooms on the Web.[3] Whether with teens or adults, freely-embraced abstinence for single people seems a much healthier way to be chaste or celibate rather than accept it as a discipline that must be practiced for fear of "sin."

Because the identification of intimacy with genitality is so common in society and because it has been overly-identified with other-imposed laws, honest efforts to explain intimacy often get sidetracked in snickers on one hand and semantics on another. This is difficult when one attempts to discuss how we celibates can be intimate; it is even more difficult when one tries to show how celibacy must be expressed in intimacy if it is to be healthy. The psychologist, Kenneth Mitchell, describes well the dilemma that occurs when a celibate is unable to discover ways to be warm and intimate with others:

> We should not be deceived, therefore, into thinking that without direct sexual expression the celibate person cannot achieve a capacity for intimacy. Nevertheless, my colleagues and I agree that almost every priest with whom we have worked, young or old, fleeing or staying, satisfied or dissatisfied, was in terms of psychological developmental issues, bothered more by intimacy problems than by problems of personal or vocational identity. The formation of priests--or nuns, for that matter--takes place in a curiously constricted world in which the opportunity to work out the meanings of intimacy for oneself is either distorted or totally lacking.[4]

2. *Celibacy as Fasting For*: Men and women who have made some kind of public profession or vow regarding celibacy have been told theirs is a very significant commitment. The significance is attributed to various ideals that have been promoted over the years to justify celibacy. Among these rationales we are told that celibacy is a way of being more available for ministry, that it signifies a commitment to some absolute, that it is a way to fulfill a ministry or that it represents the only way people can be faithful to a sense of who

they are called to be. More concretely these "purposes" might be called the functional, conditional, instrumental, developmental and witness motivations. Only one seems sufficient unto itself to represent a healthy way one might be a celibate.

The functional argument has been used for years by defenders of a celibate priesthood. Building on elements of the Pauline rationale in 1 Cor. 7, the reasoning centers on the notion that one functions better as a minister when unmarried. If you are unmarried you are more free and available to serve others. Priesthood demands total availability. Therefore priests, to be totally available, should not marry. Paradoxically the arguments are never proffered for doctors who must be "on call" at all times, or people in other professions demanding others' full access to them. Furthermore, if full functionality defines the purpose of celibacy we can ask: what happens when a celibate gets sick and cannot be available? What happens when a celibate priest retires and/or becomes unavailable for supply or help-outs? Does his celibacy then have no purpose?

A second reason proffered for celibacy might be called the conditional argument. It is required in order to do something else: i.e., to be or do this, you must be celibate. The conditional argument, despite all efforts to build it into a theology of "priestly celibacy," has proven quite futile. The old scriptural warrants have proved unacceptable and the new ones have proved to be embarrassing. That priests in other churches affiliated with the Latin Rite are married makes it clear that celibacy for priests is only a "man-made" condition.

Because of the weakness in this argument, Sandra Schneiders suggests another rationale better than but still similar to the conditional rationale: "the instrumental rationale." She explains that it is "not chosen at all but accepted as the condition for something else which seems desirable enough to warrant paying the price of celibacy." She writes:

> Some people seek membership in a community which offers solidarity in relationships and mission. Others, often homosexually oriented, seek a same-sex environment free from the stigma and violence of a homophobic society. Some

people, especially women whose feminist consciousness has been raised, need and want life companionship but have no attraction to patriarchally defined marriage. An increasing number of men and women who have completed one career and/or outlived their marriage are looking at ministry as a "second career" and religious community offers a stable and organized context for that choice.[5]

In almost every one of the examples Schneiders uses, I find some kind of community-defined rationale for the celibacy. This makes me ask: what happens when a community or even the ministry that one first embraced no longer exists? Were celibates of the nineteenth century who entered congregations geared to minister to slaves free to marry when slavery was outlawed? Were those who joined communities of celibates in the years prior to World War II to work in orphanages able to be dispensed without any guilt when those orphanages were closed? Or, what happens when the need for the ministry remains but the community no longer has the resources to support the ministry? What happens when one order, because of its decreasing numbers and unwillingness to join another, disbands? What happens when one group with one charism decides to join another group with another charism? What if you joined for the first charism and not the second? If celibacy is a charism, and the ministry no longer can continue if the charism is demanded, what is more important: the charism or the needs of the ministry? The questions are almost endless. The "instrumental" motivation for being celibate proves to be as illusory and filled with internal contradictions as the others. Yet it still is cited today as a primary motivator for people joining religious communities.

One time, when giving a talk on celibacy, I asked a group of women religious: "How many of you entered religious life for the main reason of being celibate?" Nobody raised a hand. However, one sister challenged me: "Why don't you ask: 'How many of you are now remaining in religious life for the main reason of celibacy?'" Her query suggests another rationale for celibacy; it might be termed the "developmental" rationale. According to this rationale, a person grows into his or her celibacy over a period of years. This understanding is reflected in the proverbial response of the monsignor celebrating his golden jubilee. When asked when he decided to be celibate: "I think it was last year," he answered.

I believe we all "grow into" our commitments, whether formally embraced--as in chastity or celibacy--or even less formally, as can be the case of people who don't marry who may be single or widowed. However, while this approach may have its merits, it often can contain a host of problems.

The "growing into" celibacy rationale seems to assume violations of vows and promises made in the past. It does not consider the effects of one's behavior on others who may be adversely impacted by that unintegrated behavior. And it can beg the non-celibate ways we may have lived for years previously that were discussed in chapters four and five.

The "growing into" celibacy rationale has a flip side. This happens when people "grow out of" it. Such seemed to be the case of Bishop Raymond Dumais of Gaspe, Quebec. Made a bishop in his mid-40s, he resigned in July, 2001 because of poor health arising from work pressures. In 2002 he asked for a dispensation from the priesthood so he could marry the woman with whom he had been living.

A rationale I heard about as I was in formation involved the witness-value argument. A connection is made between the early church which witnessed to faith through martyrdom and the witness of celibacy as the next best thing. The witness argument held value at one time, especially when that time was not as sex-defined as ours. However, with the media front-paging reports about ways priests and religious have violated their vows and promises from Belfast to Botswana to Boston and Luanda to Liverpool to Los Angeles, the witness arguments come across as hollow and even insincere. Today many people snicker when someone says they are going to be a priest or a religious; others wonder: "What's wrong with them" (implying some sort of sexual repression). Because some celibates--cleric or religious--have become perpetrators who have violated their fiduciary relationship not only with their victims but with the broader public, the community's trust that priests and religious have been witnessing to celibacy has been eroded seriously. Therefore, for the foreseeable future, I think we should shelf any "witness" rationale.

Despite the possible merits of the above rationales, I believe that, only when we make a clear choice from within for celibacy, for the sake of the reign of God, will we find the only motivation that makes sense and gives our lives meaning. In effect, it involves an embrace of Jesus' words about making themselves eunuchs "for the sake of the kingdom of heaven" (Mt. 19:12). It means that we "make ourselves" celibate in a way that empowers us to simply say–not as much in resignation as in gratitude: *this is who I am.*

When celibacy represents my best self, I do not "have to be" celibate; I choose it. To do or be otherwise would be to compromise my identity, myself, my "I am." The celibate choice represents the best kind of human being I think I can be.

In the end, the choice for celibacy must represent a choice freely and unconditionally made to oneself, to God and to the world. Such a celibate freely says: "Not only is this who I am; this is how I am going to be; this is the way I will relate." In other words, far from making one's self selfish or lonesome, the celibate, if s/he is going to be celibate, must become relational. This demands intimacy.

The celibate way of relating intimately represents a way free of control, manipulation, domination, exploitation or abuse. For the celibate the other is viewed as a person to be cared for with deep commitment rather than someone that can be used for pleasure. And when the situations arise in a relationship of intimacy that move one to be tempted to be genital, celibate intimacy demands of oneself a free response that closes the door to the genital way of thinking about the other, desiring the other or acting out with the other. When those situations arise, celibates–who have freely chosen to accept this "gift"–cannot find their sufficiency or an escape from it by arguing: "I can't; my vow doesn't allow it," or, "I mustn't; it wouldn't be right," or "this shouldn't be what I do here; it's against my promises," much less, "I can't; I might get caught." Rather the celibate who freely chooses to make him or herself so will say: "No, this is not who I am. I'd be misleading myself or you if I did anything but what I know I must do to remain who I am and to respect who you are."

In the last analysis, even allowing for outside forces or dynamics that close doors for us, tomorrow's celibates in the Catholic Church will be the ones who don't try to open those doors again. These celibates will be able to live with that part of their house–and their heart–intact, not ajar. Yet, because they have found ways of being warm and intimate with others, they also will have found a place in their heart only for God.

Developing Healthy Intimate Relationships

Intimacy characterizes healthy human relationships. It implies some kind of integrated emotional and personal connectedness to some other(s). Authentic intimacy demands mutual disclosure, as well as a kind of vulnerability that involves giving up the need to control. Because many people have been taught (or unconsciously choose) to deny their emotional needs and avoid relationships that might make them dependent or involve commitment, they fear intimacy's invitation at self-disclosure regarding those needs. Victor Seidler writes that this is especially true of men:

> A fear of intimacy has held men in a terrible isolation and loneliness. Often men have very few close personal relationships; we learn to live in a world of acquaintances. We grow up learning to be self-sufficient and independent, we learn to despise our own needs as a sign of weakness. Often we ask very little from others, though we do expect them to do our emotional work for us. But since we are largely unaware of these needs, we rarely appreciate others for doing this. This becomes another part of invisible female domestic labour. But since we have such little sense of our own needs, it can be difficult for us to appreciate the needs others have. This often makes us crude and insensitive in our caring for others.[6]

Achieving intimacy is virtually impossible in a culture defined by individualism since it involves relationships oriented to the other. Authentic intimacy demands healthy communication and communion among persons. It takes us beyond self into the other who reciprocates in kind. Intimacy is like a dance, I once was told. When you dance you need a partner. Without some kind of intimacy with the partner, you are merely posturing.

Authentic intimacy involves reciprocity in our self-revelation and self-donation; these become manifest in care and commitment. Committed care constitutes the core of intimacy. That's why control undermines the possibility of the intimate life. You can't control in intimacy. You can't command it. The kind of intimacy that reveals personal integration also involves something connected to freedom. To impose such a gift is a contradiction in terms. Where intimacy is forced from outside one's self–especially when it becomes part of "a package" that limits the way one can be accepted by a group--it abuses both giver and receiver. Intimacy and abuse are mutually exclusive. Given this understanding, it becomes all the more clear why imposed celibacy represents a form of abuse.

Intimacy, because it witnesses to one's love for another, is primarily relational; above all it is something spiritual. Whether it's personal intimacy, sexual intimacy or celibate intimacy, at the core of each expression something spiritual, loving and of God exists if that intimacy will be authentic. This kind of intimacy involves three inter-related levels: personal, sexual, and spousal/celibate. Sadly, the leaders of the Catholic Church seem quite paralyzed in finding and articulating ways which will ensure their solid integration. The consequence of this lack has had devastating effects. As Eugene Kennedy has written in his *The Unhealed Wound*:

> The official Church, failing to understand operationally the unity of human personality, fails also to see the unity of these issues. Pope John Paul II perceives no relationship among these issues except as fodder for the dissent that he wishes to eliminate. Yet it is the very hierarchical nature of the Church–which, in his judgment, "flows from its essence and nature"–that perpetuates the graded divisions in human personality that prevent the wound in sexuality from healing. If the official Church could admit its own discomfort with sexuality, as inseparable as the blood from the wound, and could take even a small, undefended, and therefore healthy

step toward understanding it, the priest shortage would vanish, the sacramental life of the Church as Mystery would be guaranteed, and respect for the authority of the Institutional Church would begin to rise immediately.[7]

1. *Personal Intimacy*

At the first and most basic level, we human animals are individuals. However, my particular way of being a human individual separates me from the other individuals in my genus due to the fact that I am also a person. As a person I need an identity, an awareness of who I am and how I differ from other individuals who are called this or that person. The factors that help me discover my personal identity are impacted by my family of origin, my ethnicity and culture, as well as socio-economic forces, to say nothing of my religious background with its various "shoulds" and "should-nots."

Since becoming a life-giving person involves knowing myself, identity and intimacy are interconnected. Being true to my authentic self (identity) demands healthy interaction with another (intimacy). Such intimacy involves mutual relationships defined by self-acceptance, self-disclosure and self-sharing. Indeed, the dynamic that distinguishes a human person from being just an individual like any other animal is intimacy.

Experts argue about which comes first: identity or intimacy. Some say there can be no identity without experiences of intimacy. Others say intimacy characterizes any authentic identity. Erik Erikson found intimacy connected to the task of discovering one's identity. His reasoning was quite simple: there is no chance to be intimate with another if I have not discovered and become at ease with my own identity.

It is not easy to show how identity and intimacy relate. Yet one thing is clear about any connection: there is no way one can be self-disclosing (which is the beginning of intimacy) without having some basic self-awareness. Selfhood is what makes an individual a human. Self-awareness makes a human personal. This involves some kind of relationship with other self-aware persons. Only self-aware persons can be other-aware and thus relational. Without relationality there is no intimacy.

To be able to say, "I am who I am," before I make a connection between my "self" and any role I might have (especially if I am a priest with a role of power in a church that insists priesthood itself makes me "ontologically" unique as a very special [and often isolated] "I am"), I must relate with at least some others who can also say vis-à-vis myself, "I am who I am." They must be able to do this in a way that elicits from me deep honor and respect, no matter their function in life.

How individuals become authentic persons is defined by the way we experience relationships of personal intimacy with some other(s). This level of personal intimacy represents the characteristic of a relationship of loving closeness, familiarity and friendship that is marked by mutual disclosure, struggle with differences and trust. Because personal intimacy grounds all other forms of intimacy, all definitions of intimacy must be grounded in those dynamics that constitute "personal" intimacy.

2. Sexual Intimacy

As individuals, in common with other animals, we are either male or female. But because we are humans we are persons. Consequently we are not just male and female; we are persons who are sexual by nature. Our sex will be male or female, but our personal identity (our "I am") will find our maleness or femaleness expressed in some sexual way. I cannot be who "I am" as a person without being who "I am" as male or female. However, our sexual identity goes beyond this simple identification. It not only involves our biological sex and gender, as well as the social roles and functions the culture associates with sexual identity (e.g., "a woman's place is in the home" or "big boys don't cry"). It identifies my "I am" in some sexual way that involves an attraction to the "I am" of other persons. The self-awareness of who I am as a male or female enables me to be open to the possibility of a sexual relationship with another to whom I am attracted.

In the *Times* article noted above describing the way some adults are freely embracing celibacy (at least for a time), their stories make it clear that authentic celibacy must be grounded in a healthy acceptance of one's self in relation to others. For instance, one of those quoted was Doug Carroll, a 40 year old divorced father of an 11-year old son. A features writer for *The Arizona Republic*, he recounted in a 1999 column his decision to be celibate. "Mr. Carroll views celibacy as part of a journey to self-acceptance," the article recounted. "'At midlife,' he wrote, 'I'm through apologizing for who I am.'"[8]

Self-awareness and personal intimacy enable us to discover and accept my "self" as having an individual body that is male or female with a concomitant physiology that makes me sexual. Only if an individual is personal can that one be authentically a male or female who is truly sexual-if intimacy is to characterize either level of relationships.

Sexual intimacy assumes personal intimacy. When these two dimensions are integrated, one can be an individual who is personal and at the same time a male or female who is sexual. The chart below shows how our bodily dimension is incomplete without the relational dimension which makes us capable of intimacy:

LEVELS OF INTIMACY

Bodily Dimension	Relational Dimension
Individual	Personal
Male/Female	Sexual

Within male or female genders, a person is oriented to others sexually in varying degrees on a continuum, heterosexually or homosexually. For individual males and females to be authentically personal and sexual, they must order their relationships in ways that enable them to experience and express their sexual orientation in ways that ensure intimacy.

Men, it seems, can easily confuse the need for sexual intimacy with their sexual needs and desires. Thus men often conflate intimacy with sexual contact(s). When men seek these sexual contacts primarily for pleasure, the person(s) involved can often be used (and abused) simply as objects of that pleasure. Many psychologists find in this behavior a similarity with the separation between boys and their mothers as experienced in childhood. When boys are separated from their mothers, they identify with their fathers by repressing or "cutting off" their feelings and desires. The implications for celibates is quite telling, especially when the connection between our public image and our need to control is made (especially for us males). Control "cuts off" the possibility of care; without care we are cut off from intimacy. When celibacy is mandated as a means of control by one's group, namely other clerics so-defined, the "cutting off" can become personally destructive. Consequently what Seidler writes of men in general has particular relevance for those male celibates who are not eunuchs by choice but have been "made so" by human hand:

> I think this helps explain the ease with which we "cut off" from our ongoing relationships. We have learnt to compartmentalize our feelings so that we can carefully control them. But this very "cut off" quality can hurt our developing sexual relationships and make it difficult for us to learn to take initiative and responsibility for our relationships. Often it makes our relationships incidental and our feelings unclear. Because we grow up to assume that our masculine identity has to do with our individual success and achievement in the public realm, this constantly undermines our resolve to take more initiative and responsibility in our sexual and personal relationships. Even though we are often not aware of it, we often insist on controlling the terms of relationships we are in. We get irritable if things are not done our way and we resist giving up control.[9]

Building on Seidler's thesis, it seems clear that women and men relate differently primarily because they are male and female. Men and women experience their sexuality differently (whether they are gay or straight); thus they will express it differently. A consequence of this is that the dynamics of sexual intimacy are experienced and expressed differently for men and women. Whereas women's experience of intimacy can involve a whole way of life defined by relationality, for men, intimacy usually gets compartmentalized. This leads to confusion and misunderstandings. A woman may face problems at the level of the core relationship of intimacy in not finding enough self-disclosure on the part of the man, while the man may struggle with his physiology wherein he finds the relationship moving rapidly to a very passionate level.

These differences can be alleviated with healthy, clear communication. Whatever ways women and men communicate sexually with each other, if they make an effort to understand each other–including the different dynamics they experience in the relationship--they are likely to deepen in their intimacy. Given this perspective, sexual intimacy characterizes a non-exploitative and non-genital relationship of loving closeness, familiarity and friendship that is marked by mutual disclosure, an effort to work out differences, which is expressed in affection, gestures and physical manifestations of care.

If I had to choose one word to summarize the dynamics that characterize sexual intimacy, I would use the word friendship. For years I have been fascinated by the notion of friendship, especially the fact that women and men seem to approach it differently. For men friendship seems more akin to its Aristotelian triad of being useful for each other, enjoying one another and having some common goal that bonds. While not denying these factors, women stress connectedness, belonging, continuity, trust and security as critical keys to friendships.[10]

Without denigrating the male notions of friendship, it seems to me that the feminine expression of friendship is more applicable to crossing simple male-female categories if they are to reflect sexual intimacy including self-disclosure and self-entrustment with others. Such friendship involves sharing not just one's stories but one's self. It implies being open to the other in a way that supports care and rejects control. This friendship is grounded in mutual trust and loyalty rather than manipulative individualism. Given this understanding of sexual intimacy and friendship, it's easier to see how control-defined dynamics undermine their possibility.

When celibacy is mandated it can easily become abusive both by those who demand its perpetration and those who are its victims–in themselves and in others. Eugene Kennedy compares such abuse as a kind of power to authority as "lust is to love." He explains that "those who expend it may never suspect that unacknowledged sexual need explains the complex gratification that flows from men exercising power over other men," but, he insists, this is precisely what happens when sex is subordinated to power. He explains:

> Men use power against other men in order to destroy their masculine potency. This ecclesiastical eugenics is designed to eliminate their capacity to reproduce themselves in their ideas. Feeling righteous is a totalitarian emotion and justifies wounding men in their manhood, emasculating them in the name of an institution that does not notice the shadow it casts as it focuses on and overwhelms them. Women must also be controlled and kept in their place, but men–the potent male–must be incapacitated, ruined as a man, and shamed and humiliated as well. However it has been described or in whatever supposedly spiritual disguise it appears, this movement of men to overcome other men has been profoundly sexual in its root energies.[11]

3. *Spousal and Celibate Intimacy*

Building on the above reflections, I believe that only individuals who experience personal intimacy and who, as males and females, also have relations of sexual intimacy, can experience true spousal or celibate intimacy. From everything I've said so far, it should be clear that each subsequent form of intimacy is nourished and sustained by the former. Whether individuals who are human and sexual will be authentically intimate at this third level (spousal or celibate), will depend not so much on whether they are genital or non-genital, but on whether their lives are grounded in the first two relations of personal intimacy and sexual intimacy. If their choice seems prescribed by what might be considered simply genital or non-genital, they will never be complete--just as an individual is incomplete without personal intimacy or males and females remain incomplete without sexual intimacy.

At this point, we can expand and complete the chart below in a way that includes spousal and celibate intimacy as the fullest form of intimacy, building on relational intimacy that is personal and sexual. In spousal intimacy this is genital expression; in celibate intimacy there is no genital expression.

LEVELS OF INTIMACY

Bodily Dimension	**Relational Dimension**
Individual	Personal
Male/Female	Sexual
Genital/Non-Genital	Spousal/Celibate

Considering the third level of our chart, individuals who are male and female will be genital or non-genital. Limited to the bodily dimension, a purely individualistic, simply male-female approach will find us acting genitally in an animalistic or opportunistic way. Individuals of the animal class can be genital without any intimacy. In the case of rational animals, one can be genital without sufficient consideration for the other person or consideration for being truly sexually intimate with that person. When this occurs, the "other" gets objectified and abused. S/he is viewed simply for one's pleasure, as the object upon which one can release one's sexual urges, or even for mating purposes which one views as a right. The other will be simply "useful" for one's own pleasure. Thus the other can easily not only be used, but abused as well.

Conversely, just because one is non-genital, does not automatically mean that we will be intimate. It could simply mean we have made ourselves non-genital. Our motivation may arise from depersonalizing forces like fear (i.e., of getting caught or getting AIDS) or other options discussed in chapters four and five. Such "eunuchs" who are "made so" by forces beyond their free choice won't find intimacy easily achievable.

As we consider the right side of the chart we recognize that we are also persons who are sexual. This relational capacity is the fulfillment of our bodily capacity. But we also have shown that to be fully individual we must be personal and that to be fully male or female, we must be sexual. Consequently, any integration on the third level builds on the integration of the first two levels. Our capacity to be genital enables us to be truly faithful in spousal intimacy, and our capacity to be non-genital grounds our ability to be authentically celibate. This is so whether we make a public profession to be celibate or remain celibate due to life circumstances. The conclusion of all this becomes abundantly clear: to be truly spousal or celibate, we must be fully personal as well as sexual.

Just as a person in a committed, permanent relationship involving genital expression can be faithful only if there is intimacy in that relationship and in one's relationship to God, so too people in a parallel, non-genital commitment will be chaste as long as they find ways to fulfill Fred Hickey's definition: they will be intimate in their relationships with others and God.

When God is figured into the relationship, most men and women express themselves in a genital way in accompanying forms of permanent commitment to their partner. When and where this is honored, the resulting relationship is characterized in fidelity as in the case of any biblical covenant. Expressed relationally, spousal fidelity becomes a way of intimacy with God and the other that excludes genital intimacy with anyone but the one to whom a permanent commitment has been made. Spousal intimacy can be characterized as a relationship of loving closeness and trust, familiarity and friendship that is marked by mutual disclosure, struggles with differences and acceptance expressed in affection, gestures and physical manifestations of care between two people who accept the responsibility involved in expressing their communion through genital intercourse in a permanent commitment. In its fullest sense, all spousal genital intimacy is love-making.

Just as authentic love-making is grounded in healthy spousal intimacy; love-making should characterize celibate intimacy as well.

When this happens, both spousal and celibate intimacy become manifestations of grace. They reveal God's love.

By nature, we have been made to be persons who naturally are sexual. We also have been made to be naturally oriented to express our sexual personhood through genitality. However this does not mean that every person must think, feel and act genitally in order to be an authentic person or even an authentically sexual person. Neither does it mean that we all have to be genital in order to be human, or healthy or holy. However, if we are going to be authentically sexual persons, it does imply we have found ways of being warm and intimate that are personal and sexual, even though they are not genital.

Negatively speaking, we have seen that some religious and priests use their state of "celibacy" as an excuse for not being intimate; others justify their repression of sexuality for fear of intimacy; still others engage in genital relations as an escape from intimacy. Whether one's sexuality is repressed or acted-out, all of these options, I believe, border on the abusive. And the ultimate abuse may not even be to others, but oneself.

As a result, it seems that those who act out in compulsive ways are unable to be intimate. Others manifest a sexual and/or emotional problem of some sort. Other times, as Kenel shows, the relationship can be a narcissistic one. Here the sexual partner is exploited in order to meet the celibate's own genital needs which have been wanting because of a lack of intimacy:

> These needs are not simply a matter of physical lust or sexual tension but are often related to areas of the personality that have long been buried. Because of this lack of awareness, the religious often deludes himself or herself into thinking that the problem pertains to the domain of sexuality/intimacy, when in reality the operative dynamics are on a far different level of development. To achieve integration, such persons must acquire an awareness of what it is they are seeking through their sexual behavior.[12]

Whenever publicly-professed celibates act out genitally, they have not only broken their covenant, this action indicates they have been unable, at least in that act, to integrate their sexual identity with their personal identity because the covenant that represents, at its core, a promised caring, non-genital commitment to another has been abused. Consequently and ultimately, any genital expression will be a violation of the committed celibate's sexual personhood as well. Donald Goergen writes: "Christian wisdom sees genital love as an expression of affection within a committed intimate partnership. It is precisely such partnerships or marriages that celibate men or women choose not to make. This is not to say they choose to forego intimate relationships, but intimate love need not necessarily be genital."[13]

Having recognized what dysfunctionality might result when one does not integrate the dynamics of one's bodily dimension with one's relational dimension, we can now understand more fully what it means to manifest celibate intimacy. Celibate intimacy involves relationships among those people who have committed themselves to be non-genital in response to a divine gift, a relationship of loving closeness, familiarity and friendship that is marked by mutual disclosure, struggles with differences and trust which is expressed in affection, gestures and physical manifestations of care between people. This commitment can be permanent or temporary but it is best when it is consciously chosen in one way or another. For some it may be publicly articulated; for others it will be quietly and privately accepted.

This definition of celibate intimacy is similar to the earlier definition of sexual intimacy. An important difference between them exists, however. When we speak of sexual intimacy we refer to relationships which, given the natural course of human interaction, are open to the possibility of genital expression. When we speak of celibate intimacy we mean relationships which, by the mutual consent and commitment of the persons involved, are not open to genital expression. Likewise when we speak of spousal intimacy, our definition is the same as sexual intimacy, with the exception that, in this case, the genital expression of intimacy is between partners who have committed themselves to the relationship.

Authentic celibate intimacy can be experienced or expressed when one's life is grounded in relationships that are conducive of personal intimacy and sexual intimacy. Without the first two kinds of intimacy, one will resort to genitality devoid of authentic intimacy and real commitment.

Contrary to popular opinion, the refusal to be genital without commitment is not repression. Rather it reveals an unique way of expressing love. As the late Christopher Kiesling noted, "To restrain one's desire for a physical expression of love incompatible with the loved one's celibacy (or whatever state or condition the loved one is in) shows respect for the integrity of his or her chosen way of life."[14]

Authentic celibate intimacy builds on the willingness to enter into relationships that enable an individual to be personally intimate; it enables males and females to be sexually intimate. Celibate intimacy with another or others represents personal relationships of trust and loyalty that generate the kind of caring commitment characteristic of friendship. This kind of caring commitment involves self-awareness (the personal dimension), self-disclosure (the relational dimension), self-entrustment (a trust/loyalty component) and self-commitment (the commitment component).

Here we discover how spiritual intimacy is revealed in personal intimacy. At the heart of this intimacy rests the fullest meaning of the word "faith." In other words, I believe in the other as much as I believe in myself. I have as much faith in the other to whom I am committed as I do in myself. This "faith" is what now gives my life and my relationships "meaning."

The perspective of faith makes it clear there can be no such person as a celibate without community. As should be evident as well, this community need not be geographically-defined; it all depends on one's relationships of intimacy. What this kind of community supportive of celibacy might look like will be examined later. However, as has been intimated, there can be little or no authentic faith for us if it does not ultimately find expression in spiritual intimacy. It is to this kind of intimacy that I now turn.

Spiritual Intimacy

All healthy human relationships involve intimacy of one kind or another. Authentic celibates are persons who know how to make love in the fullest spiritual sense of the term. The truly celibate person makes love, even if she or he has never had a genital experience. Having a place in their heart only for God, they love others from that place. From there they live in the reign of God.

If intimacy involves reciprocal relationships of care and commitment, only when care and commitment define the celibate choice will professed celibates be intimate. Making love involves sharing myself with another in reciprocity. Celibate and spousal intimacy are both characterized by commitment. In its spousal expression this intimacy requires a commitment to one person (the partner). By definition, that choice means a restriction of genital expression to the one who has been chosen. Such persons in committed personal and sexual relationships say by that choice they will be non-genital with anyone but the object of their commitment.

The celibate expression of this intimacy is likewise marked by commitment. On the personal and sexual level celibates pledge themselves to non-exclusive, non-genital commitments of care. Such commitments represent the only way one can reach all three levels of intimacy: personal, sexual, and celibate. When either spousal or celibate intimacy is shown in our lives, we enter a covenant of spiritual intimacy. Our relationship of loving closeness and personal familiarity with God gets expressed in ever-expanding circles of love, especially with those in need. This is another word for "compassion." At its core celibacy involves love-making (God in us) and making-love in ever widening circles (compassion for the world).

This faith perspective makes it clear that all three levels of personal, sexual and spousal/celibate intimacy assume that spiritual intimacy of some sort is providing a value-added meaning to each dimension. As an individual person, the fact that I can say "I am" mirrors that One who said, "I am,"--Yahweh. To be able to say "I am" assumes an awareness of my self as a unique person made in the image of God. But as an image of the God who is love, I can only be who "I am" if I am able to experience and express love. This involves an affective dimension that involves rapport, receptivity and reciprocity. Personal intimacy, then, is spiritual by definition.

As a sexual person, the fact that I am naturally attracted to some others reveals the constitutive attraction of the persons of the Trinity for each other. This involves a desire to be with the other and to find one's "I am" in the embrace of the other "thou." Spirituality involves sharing this level of oneself with another to become a "we." It implies intimacy that is sexual. Given this understand, Donald Goergen says we must ask how our religious identity and spiritual life are deepening in a way that impacts on the way I am sexual: "Spiritual life and sexual life interact and mature together."[15]

Finally, as a sexual person who is celibate, what makes me spiritual is the way I do not spiritualize my relationships in the sense of being removed from being sexual and personal. Rather I become intimate as a celibate precisely because I have learned non-manipulative ways of being personally and sexually caring with others. When this occurs in me my celibacy and spirituality have embraced to make me a sexually embodied person.

As a celibate, while I may be separated from other individual males and females in life by not being genital, spirituality is what enables me to make love and be a lover in a non-genital way. Making love and being in love in this way, as Jesus' enfleshment in his incarnation shows so well, is the only authentic way to be spiritual and celibate. This implies that there are covenants that are being kept.

The Communal Context: The Essential Support for the Celibate Commitment

Not expressing oneself genitally denies one's natural and human inclination. When not freely chosen it can easily make us anorexic. This, we noted above, represents the negative consequence when celibacy is limited to be a kind of fasting *from*. Its non-expression can affect us deeply, especially when we have rejected all but one of the given rationales about what we are fasting *for*.

When we do abstain from sex freely and because of an inner motivation that is identified with the deepest part of our self-identity, it is important that we find others who support, honor and/or share this approach to personal and sexual intimacy with whom we can share. If we cannot share the effects of *fasting for* something--when this affects an unnatural *fasting from*--and if we cannot *fast with* others who share the same experience, our attempt at being celibate can often become something solitary instead of a sign of solidarity. If we cannot share our struggles to be celibate, we cannot share who we are. If we cannot share in an atmosphere of confidence and trust, as well as the needs which arise from who we are as celibates, mistrust and alienation can easily occur. This demands an environment for sharing of one's self, one's faith and one's needs in a way that nourishes rather than undermines one's celibate way of life or commitment.

The new science has shown that our environment either gives energy or takes energy from its members, even when we may not be aware of this. And while a community's environment or culture might not purposely take life from its members, if it does not give life or nourish it, then it does indirectly take life by sapping the energy from them. Celibacy needs ongoing energizing if it will not end up putting us on a life-support system.

Not only do negative relationships fail to nourish our growth; they can easily undermine our personal commitments. If people have a normal need for intimacy (which rightfully must be respected and nourished in some kind of community), and if this need is not met, it is not difficult to understand why some leave the diocesan priesthood and religious life saying it no longer gives them meaning. Consequently "priests' support groups" are necessary aids in their fidelity. In the same way, groups like Dignity and Courage evidence the need of gays and lesbians for communities to support the difficulties they face in today's homophobic church and society.

Because today's societal values and mores continually erode a choice for celibacy, we find all the more need for alternative communities that reinforce celibate commitments (as well as communities related to chastity itself). One of the greatest obstacles to the development of healthy relationships of intimacy happens when we fall into patterns that are not generative of growth and reformation. When routine takes the place of surprise and rituals replace wonder, a relationship once defined by intimacy can easily begin to wane. Rather than characterizing a relationship that has become routinized as normal, being taken-for-granted in a relationship actually evidences a slow dying in the dynamics of intimacy. The result is the "you don't send me flowers" and "you don't sing me love songs" refrain all over again.

As I give workshops and retreats to priests and religious, I continually discover that many feel they can't talk to members of their households about their relationships of intimacy with others which may involve very personal and even sexual (albeit not genital) expressions. Often this occurs among priests and men and women religious in their sixties and seventies. They have finally found someone with whom they can be warm and intimate in non-genital ways. They have discovered ways they can experience and express sexual intimacy, possibly for the first time. Yet they do not feel free to share the "good news" about their relationships with those among whom they live. When I ask if they are doing anything to violate their vows or promises, or if they are abusing the relationship in any way, they always say with some degree of surprise, "Well, of course not!"

"Well why can't you share the good news of your relationship with your confreres?," I ask.

"They wouldn't understand," is what I continually hear.

Their response should make religious leaders more concerned about the lack of trust evidenced in their communities than the kind of relationships such members may have developed with their friends. This thought leads me to conclude with thoughts about the need to create covenanted "communities of entrustment" among priests and religious who choose the celibate life freely.

Building on Donald Winnicott's time-honored ideas[16] about the need to create "holding environments" or "envelopes of care," such communities will commit their members to covenant around two simple practices that all have freely chosen: affirmation and correction. In affirmation the members mutually agree to acknowledge and recognize each other as precious; in correction that flows from the affirmation members covenant to challenge each other to conversion when their ways undermine communal integrity and intimacy.

I now conclude this book as I began, recalling the founder of the community of celibates of which I am a part, Francis of Assisi. In his *Rule* he offered us–and, I hope, the whole Roman Catholic Church of Matthew 16 and Matthew 18–a beautiful vision of what a community of entrustment might look like if it is built upon those who cherish the gift of celibacy that is a mandate of the heart rather than a means of control:

> And wherever the members of the community may be together or meet each other, let them give witness that they are members of one family. And let them, in trust and loyalty, make known to each other their needs. For if a mother loves and cares for her child according to the flesh, how much more would we not love and care for each other who are brothers [and sisters] in the Spirit?[17]

Chapter Notes

[1] Erik H. Erikson, *Childhood and Society*, 35th Anniversary Ed. (New York: W. W. Norton, 1985), 264.

[2] Diana Jean Schemo, "Virginity Pledges by Teenagers Can Be Highly Effective, Federal Study Finds," *The New York Times*, January 4, 2001.

[3] Ruth La Ferla, "The Once and Future Virgins," *The New York Times*. Sunday/Styles Section, July 23, 2000. The subtitle of the article said it all: "In Some Quarters, Celibacy Is Catching On. Sex and the City? Sorry, Try a Different City."

[4] Kenneth R. Mitchell, "Priestly Celibacy from a Psychological Perspective," *The Journal of Pastoral Care* 24 (1970), 220.

[5] Sandra M. Schneiders, "Celibacy as Charism," *The Way Supplement* 77 (1993), 16.

[6] Victor J. Seidler, *Rediscovering Masculinity: Reason, Language and Sexuality* (London: Routledge, 1989),162.

[7] Eugene Kennedy, *The Unhealed Wound: The Church and Human Sexuality* (New York: St. Martin's Griffin Edition, 2002), 173.

[8] Doug Carroll, quoted in La Ferla, *Ibid.*

[9] Seidler, *Ibid.*, 174.

[10] I have found much help in understanding a feminine notion of friendship in Lillian Rubin's *Just Friends* (New York: Harper & Row, 1985). These characteristics can be found on page 18.

[11] Kennedy, *Ibid.,* 67-68.

[12] Kenel, *Ibid.*, 10.

[13] Donald J. Goergen, O.P, "Introduction," in Sheila Murphy, *A Delicate Dance: Sexuality, Celibacy, and Relationships among Catholic Clergy and Religious* (New York: Crossroad, 1992), 9.

[14] Christopher Kiesling, O.P, *Celibacy, Prayer and Friendship: A Making-Sense-Out-of-Life Approach* (New York: Alba House, 1979), 47.

[15] Goergen, *Ibid.*, 8.

[16] Donald W. Winnicot, *The Maturational Process and the Facilitating Environment: Studies in the Theory of Emotional Development* (New York: International Universities Press, 1965).

[17] This is my paraphrase of *The Rule of 1221* of St. Francis of Assisi, VI, 7-8.

DEFINITIONS

Abuse: Any way one person, group or institution uses to control (an)other(s) through fear and intimidation.

Celibacy: the embrace of a divinely offered gift inviting one to freely choose a life-commitment of abstention from genital intimacy which expresses itself in an alternate intimacy with God and others. The celibate is a person who freely embraces the divine offer to refrain from genital intercourse, who finds ways to be warm and intimate with others and who has a place in his or her heart only for God.

Celibate Intimacy: the characteristic of a relationship among people who have committed themselves to be non-genital in response to a divine gift, a relationship of loving closeness, familiarity and friendship that is marked by mutual disclosure, struggles with differences and trust which is expressed in affection, gestures and physical manifestations of care.

Church of Matthew 16: That part of the Catholic Church that is identified in its institutional expression centered in the successors of Peter and the Apostles. It is also known as the hierarchy. Sometimes it refers to the Vatican or the Curia in Rome. Often the hierarchical dimension is called "the church."

Church of Matthew 18: That part of the Catholic Church which makes the baptized a member of the Body of Christ. While all the clergy are part of this church by baptism, it usually refers to the laity.

Clericalism: The (un)conscious concern to promote the particular interests of the clergy and to protect the power (as control) and privileges that have traditionally been conceded to those in the clerical state.

Intimacy: the characteristic of a relationship of loving closeness, familiarity and friendship that is marked by mutual disclosure, struggle with differences and trust. By definition, all intimacy is personal intimacy. Thus, this definition of intimacy implies "personal" intimacy.

Power: The ability to influence. Power can be positive (through affirmation and correction flowing from it). When done so power is manifested as care. Power can be negative (through exploitation and/or domination, coercion and/or manipulation). When done so power is manifested in control.

Sexual Intimacy: The characteristic of a non-exploitative and non-genital relationship of loving closeness, familiarity and friendship that is marked by mutual disclosure, struggles with differences, which is expressed in affection gestures and physical manifestations of care.

Spiritual Intimacy: A relationship of loving closeness and personal familiarity with God that is expressed in compassion of others. At its core it is love-making (God in us) and making-love (compassion for the world).

Spousal Intimacy: The characteristic of a relationship of loving closeness, familiarity and friendship that is marked by mutual disclosure, struggles with differences and trust. It is expressed in affection, gestures and physical manifestations of care between people who accept the responsibility involved in expressing their communion through genital intercourse in a permanent commitment.

Violence: Directed power (i.e., force) that inflicts injury. Violence in any form can never be justified. It is sinful and sometimes can be a crime.